THE ARMENIAN AMERICANS

THE ARMENIAN AMERICANS

David Waldstreicher

CHELSEA HOUSE PUBLISHERS

New York   New Haven   Philadelphia

On the cover: In about 1895, Moses H. Gulesian, an Armenian immigrant, poses with his workers at the Copper and Galvanized Iron works in Boston.

Chelsea House Publishers
Editor-in-Chief: Nancy Toff
Executive Editor: Remmel T. Nunn
Managing Editor: Karyn Gullen Browne
Copy Chief: Juliann Barbato
Picture Editor: Adrian G. Allen
Art Director: Maria Epes
Manufacturing Manager: Gerald Levine

The Peoples of North America
Senior Editor: Sam Tanenhaus

Staff for THE ARMENIAN AMERICANS
Assistant Editor: James M. Cornelius
Copy Editor: Terrance Dolan
Deputy Copy Chief: Ellen Scordato
Editorial Assistant: Theodore Keyes
Picture Research: PAR/NYC
Assistant Art Director: Laurie Jewell
Designer: Noreen M. Lamb
Layout: Louise Lippin
Production Coordinator: Joseph Romano
Cover Illustration: Paul Biniasz
Banner Design: Hrana L. Janto

Library of Congress Cataloging in Publication Data

Waldstreicher, David
   The Armenian Americans / David Waldstreicher.
      p. cm.—(The Peoples of North America)
   Bibliography: p.
   Includes index.
   Summary: Discusses the history, culture, and religion of the Armenians, factors encouraging their emigration, and their acceptance as an ethnic group in North America.
   ISBN 0-87754-862-5
   1. Armenian Americans—Juvenile literature. [1. Armenian Americans.] I. Title. II. Series.   87-35447
E184.A7W35 1989   CIP
973'.0491992—dc19   AC

CONTENTS

THE PEOPLES OF NORTH AMERICA

CHELSEA HOUSE PUBLISHERS

A
NATION
OF
NATIONS

Daniel Patrick Moynihan

The Constitution of the United States begins: "We the People of the United States . . ." Yet, as we know, the United States is not made up of a single group of people. It is made up of many peoples. Immigrants from Europe, Asia, Africa, and Central and South America settled in North America seeking a new life filled with opportunities unavailable in their homeland. Coming from many nations, they forged one nation and made it their own. More than 100 years ago, Walt Whitman expressed this perception of America as a melting pot: "Here is not merely a nation, but a teeming Nation of nations."

Although the ingenuity and acts of courage of these immigrants, our ancestors, shaped the North American way of life, we sometimes take their contributions for granted. This fine series, *The Peoples of North America*, examines the experiences and contributions of the immigrants and how these contributions determined the future of the United States and Canada.

Immigrants did not abandon their ethnic traditions when they reached the shores of North America. Each ethnic group had its own customs and traditions, and each brought different experiences, accomplishments, skills, values, styles of dress, and tastes in food that lingered long after its arrival. Yet this profusion of differences created a singularity, or bond, among the immigrants.

The United States and Canada are unusual in this respect. Whereas religious and ethnic differences have sparked intolerance throughout the rest of the world—from the 17th-century religious wars to the 19th-century nationalist movements in Europe to the near extermination of the Jewish people under Nazi Germany— North Americans have struggled to learn how to respect each other's differences and live in harmony.

Millions of immigrants from scores of homelands brought diversity to our continent. In a mass migration, some 12 million immigrants passed through the waiting rooms of New York's Ellis Island; thousands more came to the West Coast. At first, these immigrants were welcomed because labor was needed to meet the demands of the Industrial Age. Soon, however, the new immigrants faced the prejudice of earlier immigrants who saw them as a burden on the economy. Legislation was passed to limit immigration. The Chinese Exclusion Act of 1882 was among the first laws closing the doors to the promise of America. The Japanese were also effectively excluded by this law. In 1924, Congress set immigration quotas on a country-by-country basis.

Such prejudices might have triggered war, as they did in Europe, but North Americans chose negotiation and compromise, instead. This determination to resolve differences peacefully has been the hallmark of the peoples of North America.

The remarkable ability of Americans to live together as one people was seriously threatened by the issue of slavery. It was a symptom of growing intolerance in the world. Thousands of settlers from the British Isles had arrived in the colonies as indentured servants, agreeing to work for a specified number of years on farms or as apprentices in return for passage to America and room and board. When the first Africans arrived in the then-British colonies during the 17th century, some colonists thought that they too should be treated as indentured servants. Eventually, the question of whether the Africans should be viewed as indentured, like the English, or as slaves who could be owned for life, was considered in a Maryland court. The court's calamitous decree held that blacks were slaves bound to lifelong servitude, and so were their children.

America went through a time of moral examination and civil war before it finally freed African slaves and their descendants. The principle that all people are created equal had faced its greatest challenge and survived.

Yet the court ruling that set blacks apart from other races fanned flames of discrimination that burned long after slavery was abolished—and that still flicker today. The concept of racism had existed for centuries in countries throughout the world. For instance, when the Manchus conquered China in the 17th century, they decreed that Chinese and Manchus could not intermarry. To impress their superiority on the conquered Chinese, the Manchus ordered all Chinese men to wear their hair in a long braid called a queue.

By the 19th century, some intellectuals took up the banner of racism, citing Charles Darwin. Darwin's scientific studies hypothesized that highly evolved animals were dominant over other animals. Some advocates of this theory applied it to humans, asserting that certain races were more highly evolved than others and thus were superior.

This philosophy served as the basis for a new form of discrimination, not only against nonwhite people but also against various ethnic groups. Asians faced harsh discrimination and were depicted by popular 19th-century newspaper cartoonists as depraved, degenerate, and deficient in intelligence. When the Irish flooded American cities to escape the famine in Ireland, the cartoonists caricatured the typical "Paddy" (a common term for Irish immigrants) as an apelike creature with jutting jaw and sloping forehead.

By the 20th century, racism and ethnic prejudice had given rise to virulent theories of a Northern European master race. When Adolf Hitler came to power in Germany in 1933, he popularized the notion of Aryan supremacy. "Aryan," a term referring to the Indo-European races, was applied to so-called superior physical characteristics such as blond hair, blue eyes, and delicate facial features. Anyone with darker and heavier features was considered inferior. Buttressed by these theories, the German Nazi state from

1933 to 1945 set out to destroy European Jews, along with Poles, Russians, and other groups considered inferior. It nearly succeeded. Millions of these people were exterminated.

The tragedies brought on by ethnic and racial intolerance throughout the world demonstrate the importance of North America's efforts to create a society free of prejudice and inequality.

A relatively recent example of the New World's desire to resolve ethnic friction nonviolently is the solution the Canadians found to a conflict between two ethnic groups. A long-standing dispute as to whether Canadian culture was properly English or French resurfaced in the mid-1960s, dividing the peoples of the French-speaking Quebec Province from those of the English-speaking provinces. Relations grew tense, then bitter, then violent. The Royal Commission on Bilingualism and Biculturalism was established to study the growing crisis and to propose measures to ease the tensions. As a result of the commission's recommendations, all official documents and statements from the national government's capital at Ottawa are now issued in both French and English, and bilingual education is encouraged.

The year 1980 marked a coming of age for the United States's ethnic heritage. For the first time, the U.S. Census asked people about their ethnic background. Americans chose from more than 100 groups, including French Basque, Spanish Basque, French Canadian, Afro-American, Peruvian, Armenian, Chinese, and Japanese. The ethnic group with the largest response was English (49.6 million). More than 100 million Americans claimed ancestors from the British Isles, which includes England, Ireland, Wales, and Scotland. There were almost as many Germans (49.2 million) as English. The Irish-American population (40.2 million) was third, but the next largest ethnic group, the Afro-Americans, was a distant fourth (21 million). There was a sizable group of French ancestry (13 million), as well as of Italian (12 million). Poles, Dutch, Swedes, Norwegians, and Russians followed. These groups, and other smaller ones, represent the wondrous profusion of ethnic influences in North America.

Canada, too, has learned more about the diversity of its population. Studies conducted during the French/English conflict showed that Canadians were descended from Ukrainians, Germans, Italians, Chinese, Japanese, native Indians, and Eskimos, among others. Canada found it had no ethnic majority, although nearly half of its immigrant population had come from the British Isles. Canada, like the United States, is a land of immigrants for whom mutual tolerance is a matter of reason as well as principle.

The people of North America are the descendants of one of the greatest migrations in history. And that migration is not over. Koreans, Vietnamese, Nicaraguans, Cubans, and many others are heading for the shores of North America in large numbers. This mix of cultures shapes every aspect of our lives. To understand ourselves, we must know something about our diverse ethnic ancestry. Nothing so defines the North American nations as the motto on the Great Seal of the United States: *E Pluribus Unum*—Out of Many, One. ⬿

Mount Ararat is Armenia's most revered landmark. In the foreground stands the Khorvirap temple, built in the 13th century.

THE PEOPLE OF ARARAT

The history of America is best seen as an ongoing process of world making. For almost 400 years men and women have departed native soil to establish a life here, in the "new" world. They have come for many reasons—to earn better wages, to attain freedom of worship and belief, and to gain rights of citizenship denied them in their homeland. Arrivals and adjustments are the peculiar mortar of the nations of North America, and the builders have come from all over the world, retaining their own shape while making essential contributions to the grand design. To learn about the immigrants, old and new, is to learn about America.

Today more than 600,000 Armenians live in the United States; another 50,000 live in Canada. Most are descendants of the 100,000 Armenians who came to America between the years 1880 and 1924. The largest concentrations of Armenian Americans live in or near those regions where their parents or grandparents settled: New England (especially Massachusetts); New York, New Jersey, and Pennsylvania; California (where more than one-fourth of Armenian Americans now live); and the Great Lakes states of Michigan, Ohio, Illinois, and Wisconsin.

Though sometimes mistaken for Turks or Greeks, or simply lumped together with all other "foreigners," Armenian Americans retain a distinct identity. This identity has its roots in the long history of Armenia, a land marked by centuries of persecution and hardship.

An Ancient Land

Armenia today is a small province in the southwestern Soviet Union known officially as the Armenian Soviet Socialist Republic. But this state occupies only a fraction of the lands that once formed Armenia. Ancient Armenia, in western Asia, included lands lying south of the Black Sea, the Caucasus mountain range, and the Caspian Sea, and east of the region known as Asia Minor, the site of modern-day Turkey. Armenia's most famous landmark, Mount Ararat (16,946 feet high), rises just west of Soviet Armenia. This mountain, identified as the landing place of Noah's Ark in the Bible's Book of Genesis, stands as a timeless symbol of the Armenians' survival as a people.

A mountainous land (the average elevation is 5,000 feet), Armenia contains many rivers, valleys, and high plains, making for a fertile terrain rich in minerals. The

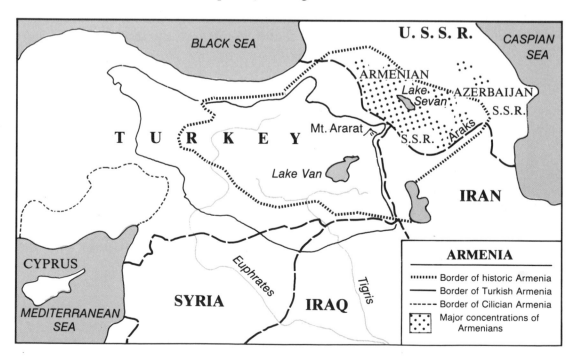

ARMENIA
- ▪▪▪▪▪▪ Border of historic Armenia
- ——— Border of Turkish Armenia
- - - - - Border of Cilician Armenia
- ▫▫▫ Major concentrations of Armenians

These figures were created during the Urartu period—about 2,500 years ago.

success of farming and animal husbandry in the region has assured the basic self-sufficiency of the inhabitants, but it has also made Armenia a prize sought by the builders of empires. Thousands of years ago, the mountains effectively protected the Armenians from would-be invaders. Nonetheless, a great wave of invasions eventually helped form a discrete group of people known as the Armenians.

The Origins of a People

Legend and record allow us to piece together an account of the origins of the Armenian nation. The people of

This drawing from a 16th-century manuscript depicts the conversion of Tiridates III and his court by St. Gregory the Illuminator in A.D. 301.

Urartu, residents of the area near Lake Van and themselves a consolidation of older tribes, were overrun some time before the 5th century B.C. by warriors from the northwest. One of the conquering groups, known as the people of Hayassa, apparently settled in the region and mixed with the local population; since then, this community has referred to itself as the people of *Hai* and to their land as *Hayastan*. But outsiders, such as the 5th-century B.C. Greek historian Herodotus, wrote of *Armenians*, the term since used by most of the world.

Invasion initiated Armenian history and defined it for centuries to come. Even though early Armenia chose its own kings, the country succumbed to various empires, such as the Median (an ancient empire that occupied the western part of modern-day Iran), the Persian (in the 6th–4th centuries B.C.), and the Seleucid Greek (in 330 B.C.).

This last empire fell to Rome in 190 B.C., ushering in Armenia's golden age. The country declared itself free of Rome, then conquered surrounding principalities, including Syria. Armenian power peaked under Tigran the Great (95–55 B.C.) Soon the expanding Roman Empire reasserted control, but for the next 500 years Armenia retained enough freedom to develop a culture all its own.

Armenian tradition tells us that sometime after the death of Jesus Christ, the apostles Thaddaeus and Bartholomew visited Armenia and gained many converts to Christianity before they were killed by the ruling elite. Some two and a half centuries later, however, Armenia's ruler, King Tiridates III, converted to Christianity through the efforts of Gregory, a royal adviser. Armenia thus became the first nation to declare itself Christian. The successful efforts of Gregory, later canonized as St. Gregory the Illuminator, helped to define

This parchment painting shows Byzantine warriors using "Greek fire" (oil thrown and ignited) to thwart their enemies.

a distinctive Armenian identity. In the 5th century A.D., a monk and a priest invented the Armenian alphabet and inscribed the first Armenian Bible. Armenians developed their own style of church architecture, characterized by a lofty dome and an imposing cruciform structure. In A.D. 451 Armenian church leaders broke away from the Catholic hierarchy because of doctrinal disputes and later established an independent body, the Armenian Apostolic church. Since then, the church has held a central place in Armenian culture and government.

The Diaspora

At the same time that Armenia began to unify itself around its exclusive brand of Christianity, territorial struggles among surrounding powers again intruded on the nation's hopes of attaining tranquillity. In A.D. 387 the feuding empires of Byzantium (modern-day Turkey) and Persia (modern-day Iran) divided Armenia between them.

Armenians in Kharpert gather for a wedding in 1892.

In the 5th century, after the extinction of the Armenian dynasty, local lords and princes emerged as leaders in both parts of Armenia. The infighting that followed in the next century made it easy for the Arabs (newly converted to the Islamic faith) to invade and extend their domination westward. For the next several hundred years, Armenia, in the words of the historian David Marshall Lang, was caught "between Byzantium and Islam." Keenly feeling the pressure, Armenians established colonies in western Asia Minor, the Balkans, and the region east of their homeland. When the Seljuk Turks began to invade ancient Armenia in the 11th century, hundreds of thousands of Armenians—perhaps half the population —migrated to Cilicia, a province in southern Asia Minor adjacent to the Mediterranean Sea. There they declared the Kingdom of Little Armenia (Cilician Armenia).

In the 11th century, the Crusades began when the pope sent armies from Europe to recapture the holy land of Palestine from the Seljuk Turks. On their way east, the crusaders met Cilician Christians, who pro-

Armenians were permitted to carry arms for self-defense until the liberation movement of the 1890s began to alarm the Turkish government.

Armenian farmers sift wheat after harvest. Cracked and boiled wheat kernels, called bulghur, *are a staple of Armenian cuisine.*

vided them with supplies and encouragement. This meeting initiated friendly relations between the Armenians of the east and the Christians of the west, though the latter provided no assistance to the Armenians from 1000 to 1500, the darkest era of their history. During this time waves of brutal invasions by the Seljuks, the Mamelukes, and the Tatars all but wasted Armenia and caused unheralded dispersal and suffering.

The last king of Cilician Armenia died in 1375, and since then, the Armenians have been a subject people in every sense of the word. In the 16th century, eastern Armenia was again partitioned by the Turks and by the Persians; parts of both sections later came under the control of tsarist Russia. It would take a new world of clashing powers and ideas to create a new Armenia—and then only at a terrible price.

An Orphaned People

The modern era of Armenian history began with the conquest of the Byzantine Empire by the Ottoman Turks (a successor empire to the Seljuks) in the 15th century. This final set of invasions erased the last vestiges of Armenian independence. The new rulers of

Asia Minor had come to stay and introduced their own style of government. The Armenians, along with other non-Muslim religious groups within the Ottoman Empire, were categorized as separate communities, called *millets*. Permitted freedom of worship and a surprising degree of political autonomy, the Ottoman millets were headed by religious leaders, known as patriarchs, who answered to higher Turkish officials.

Subjects of Muslim Rule

Constantly engaged in wars of conquest and defense, the Ottoman rulers needed to collect a maximum of taxes. The millet system, with its limited self-government, was especially well designed for this purpose. The minorities of the Turkish empire bore a heavy burden for their few liberties, but even from the Armenian viewpoint, the millets had several beneficial effects. The chief virtue was that the Armenian Apostolic church, traditionally the focal point of Armenian culture, gained much strength by serving as the agent of social control under the Turkish sultans. The stability introduced by this well-defined and enduring form of government enabled many people to prosper without giving up Armenian ways and beliefs. Yet the very separation of Muslim from non-Muslim produced, in time, a malignant legacy. The ruling Turks used the millets as a form of segregation, locking the Armenians out of mainstream society. In large cities and tiny villages alike, Armenians lived in their own quarter. This exclusion tightened the common bonds of the conquered people, but it also fed the hatred and disgust most Turks felt toward the Christian minority in their midst. Armenians, defined as *giaour* (the unclean or the infidels), suffered periodic mob attacks (pogroms). In quieter times, official discrimination reminded Armenians of their inferior status in Muslim eyes.

Nevertheless, Armenians did not live in complete isolation. The changing demands of Ottoman society in an age of economic expansion and diversification gave

them a window to the outside world. Armenians provided a vital source of labor in port cities, and because devout Muslims viewed commerce as corrupt, Armenians, as well as Greeks and Jews, found opportunities to make large fortunes as merchants and bankers. Such success, however, often resulted in renewed discrimination.

The Influence of the West

In cities such as Constantinople and Smyrna, Armenians gained more than status and money. They became exposed to the ideas of Western society, chiefly through their business-related travels. Although the majority of Armenians remained poor farmers tied to their traditional lands, in the 18th and early 19th centuries increasing numbers of Armenians sought a European education. With the modernization of the Russian empire, Western ideas even reached "Russian" Armenians who inhabited the easternmost areas captured by the tsar from the Turks.

The most important event in what has been called "the Armenian awakening" occurred in the early 1830s, when a group of Protestant American missionaries arrived with the goal of converting the Turks to Christianity. The Americans found this too daunting a task and shifted their attention to the Armenians, whose church the missionaries criticized for being too "Catholic." The conversion of Armenians to Protestantism and their education in missionary schools provoked serious conflict within the millet until the Turkish government, under pressure from Europe and America, instructed the Armenian patriarchy to respect the rights of the Protestant evangelists and their followers. Successive decades saw scores of primary and secondary schools open, staffed by westerners. In competition, the Armenian Apostolic church opened its own free schools during the latter half of the 19th century, and education became widely available.

British policymakers, because of their economic ties to the Ottoman Empire, declined to protest Turkish atrocities. The caption for this 1895 political cartoon reads, "It's hard to have to disturb him. He's such a good customer."

An inevitable result of this revolution in education was that Armenians in the Ottoman Empire sought a system of rule that accorded with their new ideals. Armenians discovered that the freedom they lacked was enjoyed by people in other countries, such as the United States and the nations of western Europe. Their appetite for liberty grew after the successful revolt by Greek nationals against their Turkish rulers in 1822–30. Young, educated Armenians gained further inspiration as well as promises of support from their fellow Christians in Europe and Russia (known as "Uncle Christian" to some Armenians of the eastern provinces). The Armenian assembly proposed a more liberal constitution for the millet, which was approved by the Ottoman sultan in 1860 and further encouraged the nationalist movement of the Armenian people.

The Turks Crack Down

At the peace negotiations after the Russo-Turkish War of 1877–78, a delegation of Armenians lobbied hard for Armenian political autonomy. The war itself had made it equally clear that Russia desired to annex Armenia. To the Turks, Armenians no longer appeared to be the empire's "loyal millet." Instead they had become an internal threat, too geographically central to be cut loose and too large to be ignored. A new sultan, Abdül Hamid II, encouraged the Kurds (a nomadic people native to Turkey) to move into Armenian lands.

Depressed economic conditions and the worsening corruption within the Turkish government heightened the zeal of young Armenian leaders. (The empire's frequent military losses and its bungling bureaucracy earned it the nickname "the sick man of Europe.") During the 1880s and 1890s organizations such as the Armenian Revolutionary Federation (the Dashnag party) and the Social Democratic (Hunchag) party emerged. These parties aimed first to secure greater political freedom within the empire and later sought to create an independent Armenian state. Growing European support for Armenian rights, coupled with the demonstrations and intermittent acts of terrorism by party members, convinced Abdül Hamid that the "Armenian Question" would have to be answered with force.

In 1894 a revolt arising from a dispute over taxes in the eastern district of Sassoun provided the excuse for a brutal reaction by the sultan. In villages and towns prominent Armenians were executed in public view and

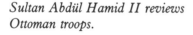

Sultan Abdül Hamid II reviews Ottoman troops.

Armenian churches and business establishments were burned to the ground. After the police had finished their work, Turkish locals had license to rampage through Armenian neighborhoods, murdering and plundering. These massacres continued for about two years, until several European nations threatened to intervene. By then, at least 200,000 Armenians had been murdered, and twice that number had been left homeless.

. . . And Armenians Rise Up

Their hopes boosted by the efforts of sympathetic outsiders, the surviving Armenian activists stepped up their drive for freedom. A successful revolution in 1908 by the Young Turks (educated nationalists who shared many ideals with the Armenian radicals), seemed at first a cause for rejoicing, but it soon became apparent that there had been no revolution in the centuries-old attitudes of the Turkish people. The militaristic nationalism embraced by Muslim leaders only excited the resentment felt by Turks against Christian minorities. Rebellions by Christians in the Ottoman-dominated Balkan Peninsula cast further doubts on Armenian loyalty. "The opinion is fostered among the Muslim masses," protested the Armenian patriarch in conjunction with the Armenian National Assembly in 1913, "that it will not be possible to preserve from European encroachment what still remains of Ottoman territory, except by annihilating the Armenian element." In the summer of 1914 the Turks entered World War I on the side of Germany and Austria-Hungary against Great Britain, France, and the other Allies. Although Armenians were drafted and served with distinction in the Turkish forces, rumors of disloyalty persisted, especially in light of the Armenians' understandable aversion to fighting the Russians. The Young Turk government resolved to use the Armenians as a scapegoat to distract the Turkish people from their own continual military setbacks and unimproved living conditions. To this end, in September 1915 the Turkish interior minister instructed a provincial governor:

> You have already been informed that the Government has decided to exterminate entirely all the Armenians living in Turkey. . . . Without pity for women, children, and invalids, however tragic the methods of extermination may be, without heeding any scruples of conscience, their existence must be terminated.

First the Armenian soldiers were disarmed and confined; later, they were marched out of town, lined up in trenches, and shot. Official demonstrations were again followed by mob massacre, but now the slaughter was not even confined to towns removed from European eyes. Throughout the empire, Armenians saw their homes ransacked and burned, and under general orders of deportation, Armenians left their places of birth and headed east, toward the desert. Hundreds of thousands died of starvation there or in refugee camps improvised in Syria, Lebanon, and other countries east of Turkish control.

Turkish authorities march Armenians out of Kharpert in 1915. Most of these men would never see their families again.

Hundreds of thousands of Armenians died of starvation and exposure after fleeing the Turkish massacres.

Their Common Tragedy

American and British relief efforts helped some to re-settle, but nothing could stem the tide of displacement and death. Of the more than 2.5 million Armenians living in the Ottoman Empire before the war, at least 1 million perished, and another million were forced to flee. Some found their way west but most remained in the Middle East and in or near what is now Soviet Armenia.

In the wake of the brutal years of 1890–1920, Armenians all over the world are tied together through the common tragedy of their violent expulsion from their ancient homeland. The murder of countless Armenians at Turkish hands is all the more disturbing because it was planned in advance by the Turkish government and largely carried out by the Turkish people. Given the horrific extent of this series of events, known collectively as the Armenian Genocide, it is not surprising that those who escaped or survived the massacres have the self-image of survivors—a state of mind that would greatly affect their experiences in a very different world.

To the NEW WORLD

Constantinople, Cilicia, Russia, and the Near East: Armenian history echoes with sagas of exodus. The presence of Armenians on every continent testifies to the recurrent need of this orphaned people for a new home. Their desire for a port of welcome did not mean, however, that they wished to erase their old identity. Armenians have scattered all over the world because of unbearable conditions in their native land. They chose America because of the special conditions of this country—making theirs both an Armenian and an American story.

In many respects the first Armenians in America resembled the first settlers of the New World: They came alone, to the wilderness, in search of fortune. The records of the Jamestown colony of Virginia (founded in 1607) refer to one "Martin the Armenian," who evidently arrived in 1619 as a bound servant. Like nearly every Virginian during those years, Martin raised tobacco and was paid for other work with the crop. In 1623, freed from servitude by Governor George Yeardly (who may have been his employer), Martin took his tobacco bounty with him back to London. There he attended several meetings of the Virginia Company of London and informed the firm's directors that he intended to return to the New World. Whether he did so is unknown; there is no record of his adventures after 1624.

Two women of Bitlis churn butter in 1900. Most Armenians, even during the Genocide years, lived in farming villages.

The early colonists' reliance on tobacco worried the colony leaders and their British sponsors. Seeking other means to ensure the survival and profit of the Virginia experiment, they attempted to grow a variety of the cash crops demanded in European markets. In 1653 a planter named Edward Diggs brought "George the Armenian" and an associate all the way from Smyrna, hoping (in vain as it turned out) to establish a native silk industry. Diggs's friends in the legislature certainly supported his efforts; they even donated 4,000 pounds of tobacco to George as an inducement "to stay in the country."

Though other Armenians may have been attracted by New World opportunities during the colonial era, there is no record of their numbers or experiences. No real Armenian community existed in America until many years later. Yet as Robert Mirak has noted in *Torn Between Two Lands: Armenians in America 1890 to World War I*, the documented existence of these 17th-century Virginian Armenians comforted later generations of Armenian immigrants. As witnesses to the earliest stages of American history, Armenians could feel as American as the first pioneers.

The Many Attractions of the New World

Like the Puritans who founded the Massachusetts Bay Colony, the first Armenians to settle in New England came for reasons of religious faith. These young men had been converted to Protestantism by the American missionaries who first worked in Turkish Armenia in the 1830s and who encouraged some Armenians to pursue their studies in American institutions of higher learning. During the next half century, about 70 English-speaking students left for the United States, usually intending to return home after a few years to fill the great need in the provinces for teachers, doctors, and other professionals. This was the first group migration of Armenians to North America.

Some of these students met with such success in the New World that they opted to remain there. One such

During the Russo-Turkish Wars, some 250,000 Armenians joined the Russian army.

immigrant, Khachadur Osganian, arrived in 1834, graduated from New York University, returned briefly to Constantinople, then sailed again for New York to work as a dual correspondent for the *New York Herald* and a Constantinople newspaper. In the following years Osganian often wrote about his delight with America and urged other Armenians to join him in the land of freedom. A highly respected journalist, Osganian served as president of the New York Press Club and in 1857 published *The Sultan and His People*, probably the first book written in English by an Armenian writer. Another young scholar, Christopher Der Seropian, introduced the yearbook at Yale University and later invented the green and black dyes still used on American paper currency.

These intrepid young men became the first to feel divided between nostalgia for their homeland and the

Armenian-Protestant ministers adopted the religion and some of the culture of American missionaries. In this photo from 1870, the younger ministers (center), who had studied abroad, no longer wear the traditional fez.

The introduction of free schools changed the lives of many Armenians in the 19th and early 20th centuries. In this photo poor children line up for new books.

excitement of living in a rapidly growing America. Some returned to staff churches, schools, and hospitals in the homeland while others remained, encouraging their countrymen to follow their path to liberty and success. Khachadur Osganian went so far as to draw up plans for an Armenian city in the American Midwest. Such ideas irked missionaries in Armenia, who thought the native-born should return to spread the biblical word locally. Fearful of losing all the young educated men of the provinces, the missionaries soon began to discourage emigration. Even so, many of their students responded to the commercial possibilities available in American cities. Armenians in Boston, New York, and Chicago—educated in missionary colleges (and sometimes brought to the United States by the Americans themselves, as servants)—pioneered the Oriental-rug trade for which Armenians are still renowned.

The Tabibian and Iskian families had a summer home in Angora (later Ankara, the capital of Turkey). Turkish-Armenian merchants and professionals often amassed considerable fortunes.

Between Two Worlds

In keeping with the overall character of Armenian migration to America, the first real wave of immigrants came as a result of worsened conditions in the homeland. In the region of Kharpert, where the Protestant mission had long been established, widespread poverty led many young men to sail for America, where jobs were available at better pay. Stories of quick riches, originating in American immigrants' letters to family and friends back home, spurred hundreds of Armenians to make the long voyage to America during the 1880s.

By 1890, about 1,500 Armenians lived in the United States. Most were poor laborers from the provinces who came searching for a better livelihood. Traditionally, job-hungry young Armenian men traveled hundreds of miles west, to Bitlis, Smyrna, and Constantinople. Once they had saved enough money, they returned to their native villages. Now they traveled thousands of miles, to America, but they did not give up the plan of eventually returning home. At least five of every six new arrivals were male, and many left families behind. With no loved ones, no church, and only a tiny community of equally dispossessed countrymen, the typical Armenian immigrant of the 1880s had little desire to make America his permanent home.

The second wave of Armenian immigration to the United States commenced in the last decade of the 19th century. Its causes, even its ebb and flow, can be traced back to the degrees of hardship experienced by the Armenians in the Ottoman Empire. Government-approved reprisals against the citizens of small eastern villages in 1890, for example, caused almost 2,000 Armenians to leave for the United States: between 1890 and 1891 the Armenian-American population doubled. In all, more than 13,000 Armenians reached the United States between 1890 and 1899, a mere trickle compared to the total world population of Armenians (about 3 million in 1900). Still, the vision of America as a promised land had begun to spread.

Why did so few Armenians book passage? One factor was the distance to the New World. It was much cheaper and easier to move east across the Russian border, as tens of thousands did before 1900. Moreover, in 1892 Sultan Abdül Hamid II placed tight restrictions on Armenian travel. Permits for journeys to the coast became notoriously difficult to obtain; the bribes necessary to reach a port and actually leave the country seemed to multiply without end. Despite these problems, the unprecedented Hamidean massacres of 1894–96 spurred an increase in migration. Many fled first to Europe, where they could more easily gain passage to America.

Like many new Americans, Armenians were eager to demonstrate their patriotism, even if it meant bearing arms for their adopted country. Melcon Mangasarian (shown here) of Providence, Rhode Island, served in the Spanish-American War.

Though the sprees of looting and killing eventually subsided, the economic situation in the Ottoman Empire worsened in the chaos of the massacre years. Even when trade returned to its normal level, Armenians knew that riots might begin again at any time. "We Armenians lived in an atmosphere of suspense and conspiracy," wrote Sarkis Torossian, a captain in the Turkish forces. "It was like living in a beleaguered city, in an armed camp, only there were no arms. . . ," for Armenians were not allowed to keep weapons of any kind. Under such conditions, rich and poor alike dreamed of leaving the land of their fathers to secure a better life for their children.

An average of 1,500 Armenians arrived in the United States annually during the first 6 years of the 20th century. During the next two years, the annual figure nearly doubled. Chain migration increased in earnest: naturalized Armenian immigrants were writing home, sending money, advising relatives and friends about work opportunities, and often buying steamship tickets for their loved ones to join them. Whole families began to immigrate. "American fever" was no longer a fad of youth; it was the one great chance for all.

The Darkest Years

The next surge in immigration took place after the Young Turk Revolution in 1908. The reforms promised and implemented by the new regime included lifting restrictions on movement within and from Turkey. As conditions improved, the issue of immigration became tied to the issue of loyalty. The Dashnags insisted that Armenians should remain and help build a new Armenia; others thought it foolish not to seize the chance to leave for greener shores. Many Armenians simply did not care to be part of a new Turkey, especially if it meant forced service in the Ottoman Army. The Cilician massacres of 1909, in which 30,000 perished, proved further that Armenians faced serious danger, and immigration to the United States soon reached new heights: 5,500 in 1910 and more than 9,000 in 1913. The beginning of World War I abruptly halted this era of spiraling migration, during which a total of 66,000 Armenians had come to America. By late 1914, travel was forbidden to all non-Muslims.

When the systematic program of genocide began in earnest, Armenians were lucky to escape Turkish lands with their lives. Only a few thousand reached North America during the war years, while more than 1 million of their countrymen were being slaughtered by the Ottoman Turks. When the Ottomans seemed on the verge of losing the war in 1918, Armenians on the eastern frontier rose in revolt and won their independence. The short-lived Republic of Armenia (1918–20) held elections and absorbed hundreds of thousands of Armenians from all over the Near East before the revitalized Soviet Union, with the acquiescence of the Turkish government, invaded the small landlocked territory and toppled the Armenian government. Thereafter a flood

Women and children were often the only survivors of families attacked during the massacres.

of refugees (some 30,000 in 5 years) arrived in the United States and Canada, mainly women and children who had lost their male relatives in the massacres. A much larger number wanted to come to America but lacked the financial means.

The narrow escape of many Armenians caused them to reflect with disbelief on the ordeal they had weathered. Abraham Hartunian, a priest in training, came so close to being killed in the massacres that he saw the hand of God in his survival and safe passage to America. The memoirs of the survivors are filled with amazed suppositions: "If that Turk had not given us back our wagon. . . ."; "If the [official] had not taken our bribe. . . ." Only the timely intervention of a member of the American Near East Relief Committee saved George Mardikian, a soldier in the short War of Armenian Independence, from starving in a Turkish prison camp.

Other Perils of the Trek

If Armenians safely reached a port city they faced the unsettling boat ride across the Atlantic. "Two or three hundred of us were crowded like cattle in the gloomy hold" for 12 long days, wrote one immigrant. "We had no berths." Kaloost Nazarian lamented that his wife, who was accustomed to having servants at her call, now had to travel in steerage. "We who were in the lower berths or bunks got all the lice and bedbugs that rained down from above."

Other anxieties plagued the voyagers. Even if they had passports and the requisite funds, immigrants had no guarantee that they would be admitted: Once in port, their fate rested in the hands of immigration officials. Families, such as Kerop Bedoukian's, were often temporarily split because one or more member had contracted trachoma, a contagious eye disease. After 1897, it was illegal for the shipping lines to transport aliens with trachoma; thousands had to delay their trip in Eu-

The establishment of Armenian churches in America was truly a communal endeavor. The Holy Cross Armenian Apostolic Church of West Hoboken (now Union City), New Jersey, was consecrated in 1906.

rope to seek treatment. There was often the fear that one might contract the disease on board ship or suffer a relapse. In all, though, only about four percent of the Armenians who arrived in New York were denied entry to the United States.

For about 30 years, America annually received a growing number of Armenians fleeing the oppression of their homeland. The path and their reception in the New World were often circuitous, but their much-tested sense of survival carried most of them through. The same spirit, free of many old social and political constraints, would help them start anew.

The passage of the Johnson-Reed Immigration Act of 1924 effectively closed the door against further Armenian immigration to the United States. This law, inspired by America's growing fears of unassimilated "foreigners," established a quota system by which the total number of immigrants permitted entrance each year could not exceed 150,000, with the number al-

Some immigrants hoped to found a "New Armenia" in the American West. The Kevorkian-Bogdasarian family posed for this photograph in 1885 on their way to Texas.

lowed each nationality based on its total population already living in America. The Johnson-Reed Act intentionally favored long-standing and large ethnic groups, such as the Germans, English, Irish, and Scandinavians (all from western Europe), and was a disadvantage to natives of Asia and eastern Europe who had begun to immigrate to America more recently. Annual immigration of Armenians dwindled to the hundreds, and a chapter in the Armenian-American experience closed.

Reaching the Gate

For the 100,000 Armenians who came to America before 1925, passage to the New World was no simple act:

It was an ordeal of helplessness undertaken amid unforeseen difficulties. The first and perhaps most daunting obstacle was the cost. The price of a steamship ticket, which was between $25 and $35, seems a bargain today, but in 1900 this sum represented half the yearly income of an unskilled Turkish laborer. Moreover, local officials demanded bribes of as much as $20 for *teskeres* (passports) to the port cities on the Mediterranean and the Black seas. The poorer farmers made these trips of hundreds of miles on foot, in groups of 40 or more. They surrounded themselves with a caravan of wagons meant to afford protection, but, in fact, were vulnerable to attack on open roads by Turkish and Kurdish marauders. When parties of migrants reached the seaports, they encountered "agents" (often Armenians themselves), who made their living by securing lodgings or making travel arrangements for prospective immigrants. Many could afford passage only to cities such as Smyrna, Constantinople, and Marseilles, and thus had to stop for months in order to find jobs and earn the money to proceed further. For some it took years to complete the journey to the promised land.

Those who succeeded in reaching America, especially in the early years, belonged to "the comparatively well-to-do," as one contemporary phrased it. Even for these fortunate ones, escape might not have been possible had not relatives sent money, in the form of traveler's checks, from the New World. Indeed, an increasing number of tickets were purchased in advance by Armenian Americans: The proportion of immigrants with prepaid tickets reached one in three before the war. ∾

*At Ellis Island, in New York
Harbor, newcomers anxiously
awaited official admittance to
the United States.*

MAKING A HOME

The surge in Armenian immigration beginning in the 1890s was an increase both in number and kind. Unlike the first arrivals, these newcomers often intended to stay in the United States at least until the establishment of a truly free Armenia. Optimistic letters from the Armenian expatriates established America in the mind of Armenians back home as a land of freedom and prosperity. The massacres of 1894–96 and 1909 accelerated the spread of "American fever." By the postwar period of immigration, 90 percent of the new arrivals could name the home of a friend or relative as their specific destination.

First Days . . . and Setbacks

Upon landing at Ellis Island, the brave young men and women knew nothing of America save what they had heard from fellow countrymen. Few had any guarantee of employment, and fewer still could speak English. Whenever possible, they made their initial contacts with friends and relatives. In this way a community took root: Armenians stayed together because they needed each other in a strange, if relatively benevolent, new land.

The costs of the journey were so great that most immigrants arrived with only a small sum in their possession. Thus the first order of business for the "greenhorn," or new immigrant, was to find work. After passing through customs and receiving immigrant alien papers, the newcomer usually traveled by train to meet the friends or family members who had helped arrange the great move. Some were lucky enough to have jobs secured for them in advance, in which case they proceeded directly to their future place of employment.

Not all were this fortunate. Those who fled in the face of official deportations and the lightning destruction of homes and villages rarely had the time or wherewithal to make such arrangements. Other immigrants, such as the Jews, Germans, or Italians, could look to a large community for help, but Armenians were not as large or visible a minority. Recognizing this, several wealthy Armenian Americans enlisted the support of some American humanitarian groups—including the Boston-based Friends of Armenia—and collected donations to aid the thousands fleeing the Hamidean massacres of 1894–96. The success of these efforts inspired the creation, in 1900, of the Armenian Colonial Association. This agency eventually hired agents to help Armenian immigrants at Marseilles, France; New York, and Chicago. Thousands of Armenians got their first jobs through the intervention of this organization.

After immigrants were inspected and registered, they were ferried to Manhattan, thus receiving their first glimpse of an American city.

Into the New Industries

Though nearly all immigrants at the turn of the century disembarked at the port of New York, it would have been beyond the capacity of even that swelling metropolis to house and sustain such vast numbers of newcomers. Where exactly did the Armenians go? Most followed their predecessors to places with available jobs. The factory and mill towns of the Northeast and Midwest became the sites of the Armenian-American communities of the New World. New methods and machinery permitted a phenomenal expansion in the clothing and steel industries, among others, in the latter part of the 19th century. Inexpensive labor was needed to run the new factories, and the great waves of immigrants of the generation before World War I largely filled this need. The United States could never have become a great industrial power without the millions of Old World immigrants who supplied the muscle for the push into the 20th century.

The new industries ideally suited the large wave of Armenian immigrants, often grown men willing to travel to unheard-of places for the best wages and lowest living expenses. In doing so, they could save money to send home to dependents. Some already possessed knowledge of business and manufacturing: Armenians had traditionally been the merchants of the Ottoman Empire. These young immigrants carried the recent memory of an uneasy life among the Turks. "Years of oppression and struggle for existence," wrote M. Vartan Malcolm in 1919, "has made them accustomed to hard work." Armenians readily endured long hours in factories, tanneries, coal mines, and stockyards in order to secure freedom for themselves and their families.

Good Wages and a Rude Awakening

By our standards, the wages offered for unskilled hands in the new industries seem meager. But compared to what Armenians had come to expect in economically

Like two of the first Armenians to visit North America, these later immigrants manufactured silk. Armenian Americans often worked in the expanding textile industries.

depressed Turkey, beginners' pay of one to two dollars per day was, in fact, a real incentive. Word of specific opportunities spread quickly. In 1887 about 400 Armenians lived and worked in Worcester, Massachusetts; only 9 years later, the Armenian-born population there surpassed 1,000. A great number of these immigrants worked in the Washburn & Moen wire factory. The company president (a former missionary) encouraged Armenian laborers to write home about the "generous" terms of labor in Worcester. The resulting tide of newcomers made Worcester the first center of Armenian life in the United States.

Similar developments occurred in factory towns all over the Northeast around the turn of the century. The Hood Rubber Company of Watertown, Massachusetts, attracted hundreds of Armenians. Shoe factories and metalworking plants in Boston and the nearby cities of Lynn, Chelsea, and Cambridge also became havens for new arrivals. Wherever new industries boomed, Armenians congregated: Hartford and New Haven, Connecticut; Providence and Pawtucket, Rhode Island; Lawrence and Lowell, Massachusetts; Camden and

Paterson, New Jersey. To the Armenians of eastern Turkey, these magically foreign names meant prosperity, security, and amity.

The few Armenian women who worked outside the home usually found jobs at the textile mills or garment shops in the Northeast or in the fruit-packing houses in California's San Joaquin valley. In Troy, New York, scores of them were employed in a shirt-collar factory; they also took home piecework and sewing, like many other immigrant women. For both sexes, this new world of work offered many hardships. Labor conditions in the factories often proved shocking and almost always disappointing. Employees toiled more than 50 hours per week, sometimes as many as 70, in order to earn a $9 paycheck. The tasks themselves, though not always backbreaking, could be boring and repetitive. Immigrants reported feeling like mere extensions of the quick-moving, endlessly active machines they operated.

The growth of Armenian-American communities enabled some new arrivals to start small businesses or enter the service professions.

Many looked back longingly to a youth spent on the farms of the Armenian plains: There at least one knew sunlight and fresh air. A high rate of job turnover characterized this era, as industrial workers sought less tiresome means to earn a decent wage.

Fighting the Factory Wars

Despite the turnover, jobs could be hard to find. The high tide of immigration in the 1890s and 1900s (a total of 12.5 million immigrants came to America during these two decades) resulted in periodic labor gluts. The severe economic slump of 1894 put an estimated 25 percent of American workers out on the street, and immigrants were always the first to be laid off. Some Armenian newcomers resorted to bribing factory foremen for jobs—a practice distressingly reminiscent of corruption in the old country. Others did not realize that the wages they gladly accepted fell below the normal rate. This situation compounded the immigrants' difficulties because many American-born workers came to resent the foreigners who worked for less.

Some Armenian Americans damaged their reputation further by occasionally agreeing to act as *scabs*, or strikebreakers. When fledgling unions went on strike, management sometimes hired experienced Armenians to find newly arrived countrymen to replace the strikers (many of whom were themselves immigrants). The resulting tensions between ethnic groups—Irish versus Armenians in Massachusetts, for example—form a sad but true chapter in the immigrant experience.

Job shortages in the Northeast sent thousands of Armenian Americans to the cities of the Midwest, which allegedly offered better wages and working conditions. Soon there were flourishing Armenian communities in Detroit, Chicago, Milwaukee, and Waukegan, as word spread in the East and to the old country of opportunities in the developing steel and auto industries.

(continued on page 57)

PASSING THE TORCH

Overleaf: *The color and expressiveness of an old-country dance live again at an Armenian-American parade.*

Left: *Christianity came to Armenia in the 4th century and has been practiced ever since in both Armenian and American settings. Above: A priest washes a boy's feet during a Holy Week service at the St. Vartan Armenian Cathedral in New York City.*

Left: *Long known for the manufacture and retail of fine Persian and oriental rugs, Armenians chafe against the "rug merchant" stereotype.* Above: *Kevork Ourfalian poses in his bakery and provisions store.*

The darkest moment in Armenian history was the slaughter of more than 1 million Armenians by the Turkish government in 1915. Left: The memory of this tragedy is underscored at an annual Armenian Martyrs' Day march by paraders who drag the Turkish flag through the street. Right: In recent decades, descendants of immigrants have found common ground with newly arrived refugees from Soviet Armenia in proudly proclaiming, "I am Armenian."

At a political rally in New York City's Central Park, priests (front) join thousands of other marchers who raise the colors of the Armenian flag. Many members of the community hope that some day Armenia will again become an independent nation.

(continued from page 48)

On the whole, Armenians fared well as factory laborers. Statistics compiled in 1904 show that the average yearly earnings of Armenian industrial workers in Massachusetts exceeded the average for other recent immigrant groups. A lifetime of adversity and the need for money to send to loved ones overseas may have given Armenians both the ability and cause to work extraordinarily hard. Most of them, it should be noted, saw such work as a temporary expedient. A proportionately high number had been merchants or professionals in their native land, so it was only natural for them to seek a different life than that of the ill-paid, ill-housed industrial worker.

At first many Armenians expected to return to their home villages as knowledgeable and skilled men of the world. Later they planned to enter trade or service professions on their own terms in America. As their communities grew, Armenians successfully opened groceries, tailor shops, general stores, and restaurants. Street-smart entrepreneurs doubled as legal advisers and travel agents, providing any number of services for fellow immigrants. The best opportunities for self-employment existed in the areas with the greatest concentration of Armenians (such as Worcester), and the larger cities (such as New York, Philadelphia, and Bos-

Armenian immigrants traveled widely in search of industrial jobs. By 1913 many had found their way to Detroit and its steel foundries.

ton). By the time World War I began in 1914, more than half the Armenian men employed in Boston owned or worked in a small business establishment.

Adding to the Larger Community

The rich cultural diversity of America is the result of contributions by immigrants from all over the globe who have brought new customs and goods to the United States. In doing so they have often created a niche for themselves. A particular contribution of the Armenians in America is the introduction and popularization of Oriental rugs. The first Armenian-American dealer in this Middle Eastern specialty was Hagop Bogigian, a student of the Protestant missionaries of Kharpert who, after a falling out with his religious superiors, decided to enter business instead of the priesthood. Starting with a few rugs in the corner of a Harvard Square shoe store in Cambridge in 1881, Bogigian found success when his first customer, the poet Henry Wadsworth Longfellow, spread the word to friends about this new-comer and his carpet establishment. Within a few years

Hagop Bogigian pioneered the Oriental rug trade in Boston. His downtown store (at the corner of Beacon and Park streets) remained a landmark for many years.

Bogigian was selling imported Persian rugs to the upper crust of Boston, earning enough profit to establish a shop downtown. Later, experienced Armenian merchants from Constantinople expanded their operations to the cities of New York and Chicago. These ventures met with unparalleled success and enabled wealthy tradesmen to encourage the charitable efforts of the Armenian-American community on behalf of their suffering countrymen.

Capitalizing on the growing popularity of the "imported Oriental," some Armenians entered carpet manufacturing and contributed much to that new industry. The renowned Karagheusian family built a factory in Freehold, New Jersey, that enabled them to produce relatively inexpensive domestic Persian rugs, thereby making the exquisite Oriental designs affordable to many more Americans. Armenians also made inroads in the related businesses of rug cleaning and repair. Over time, carpet entrepreneurs enticed more than a few Armenian Americans away from sweatshops operated by American-born owners.

The Fruits of Life in California

Knowledge of trade was not the only Old World legacy to shape the Armenian communities. Armenia is a fertile country where a great many worked the soil for their sustenance. Many of the new immigrants dreamed of owning their own farms in America, a land free of raiding Kurds and leeching taxation. Some of them got their chance in the unclaimed San Joaquin Valley of central California. The first Armenians to arrive there were the Seropian brothers, formerly of Worcester. Drawn west by the favorable climate, they opened a general store and eventually entered the fruit-packing business. In their letters home, the brothers bragged of their financial success and the bounty of the irrigated San Joaquin. As a result, a group of 40 Armenians left Marsovan in 1883 to help pioneer this promised land for their people.

The laborious chore of picking and drying grapes enabled many Armenians of the San Joaquin Valley to gain a foothold in the New World.

The first years of the 20th century witnessed rapid growth in this new Armenian community. The "little Armenia" near the Fresno railroad tracks grew and spread: In 1900 the population stood at 500; in 1908 it had increased to 3,000; and by 1914, 10,000 Armenians resided in Fresno County. Flight from the old country played a role, but the exodus came mostly from the industrial towns of New England. The lure of the agricultural life, combined with the existence of a thriving Armenian community, prompted both solitary males and whole families to go west. For many the climate itself was sufficient attraction. The valley, as one veteran of Cambridge winters put it, "was so much like our homeland."

Scrupulous saving enabled many of the new westerners to put a down payment on a farm or vineyard. Inevitably, Armenians made their own contribution to viticulture (the raising of vine crops) in the region. Malcolm G. Markarian was the first to successfully market native-grown figs; Krikor Arakelian became "the melon king of America." The most widespread enterprise, cultivating grapes for raisins, attracted many California Armenians. Those who did not own or lease land usually started as farm laborers, harvesting and drying the grapes. Others, especially the women, worked in the packinghouses, often for fellow Armenians, under conditions that at times hardly differed from the steaming halls of the East Coast textile mills.

Dependence on a primary crop had drawbacks: The prosperity of the entire community could hinge on the nationwide demand for raisins. Efforts at organizing the raisin growers in order to control crop volume and prices achieved some success, but unpredictable slumps occurred nonetheless. Even the "Sun Maid Raisin Association," as William Saroyan reminisced in his 1934 short story "Raisins," could not tame the vagaries of the marketplace:

> All over our valley we were eating raisins because we couldn't sell them. People couldn't buy raisins because they were a luxury, and we had to eat raisins because they were a luxury.

Despite the hard times, Saroyan considered Fresno a nourishing home for the dispossessed of Armenia. "Standing at the edge of our city," he wrote in the same story, "a man could feel that we had made this place of streets and dwellings in the stillness and loneliness of the desert, and that we had done a brave thing. . . . We were slowly creating the legend of our life."

Solidarity and Citizenship

Soon Fresno had the highest concentration of Armenians in the country, second in total number only to New York. For those who wished to recreate Hayastan in the fertile San Joaquin Valley, this progress gave them a chance to go back in time; but some Fresno natives feared the competition of the enterprising Armenian Americans and discriminated against them. "Every act of an Armenian became conspicuous," wrote Charles Mahakian, a Fresno native, in *History of the Armenians in California* (1935). American churches and fraternal societies excluded Armenians from membership. Restrictive land covenants (clauses in contracts forbidding sale or lease to members of specified racial or ethnic groups) froze Armenian Americans out of desirable neighborhoods. "One way or another," wrote the journalist Ben Bagdikian, "every member of 'the foreign element' felt the contempt in personal relations, in traumatic experiences in school, in barriers to jobs.'' Most minority groups in America have suffered such treatment. Indeed, Armenian Americans have been spared the worst manifestations of bigotry. Even in Fresno, racism affected them less than other groups, as Armenians were considered less "different," and thus less threatening, than the Japanese and Chinese immigrants.

One way for Armenians to escape bigotry was to adopt U.S. citizenship. The benefits of naturalization included more than just a legal document and the right to vote: Citizenship solved a host of potential legal and work-related problems facing the immigrant alien. Moreover, those with full rights found it easier to help their relatives abroad. Until 1908, only the families of American citizens could legally emigrate from Turkey. For these reasons, thousands of Armenians born in the old country took and passed the required tests and received their citizenship papers.

Yet more potential citizens held back. As long as there was hope for a free Armenia, some considered it a betrayal to renounce the homeland. To George Mardikian, a veteran of the War of Armenian Independence, this argument amounted to "accepting all the advantages of America, without accepting any of the responsibilities of citizenship or loyalty." Taking great pride in his status as a "citizen by choice," Mardikian remarked sadly on the "funny, childish pride" of those ashamed to admit their alien status and of those who feared "the questions of the naturalization examiner." It is certain, though, that many of those who declined to file for citizenship were ineligible, because in 1919, 40 percent of the Armenian Americans could not read or write English with any proficiency.

Nativism, a widespread belief that only members of the "old stock" of America could be genuine citizens, endangered the efforts of Armenians to achieve naturalized status. In 1909, an official of the Bureau of

Armenians brought from the old country a knowledge and appreciation of fresh produce.

Naturalization claimed that Armenians belonged to "the yellow race" and as such were ineligible for citizenship. Although the federal court in Massachusetts ruled that Armenians were Caucasians of European origin, the same issue arose again in 1924 when a Portland rug merchant named Tateos Cartozian was denied his papers on the grounds that he was an Asian, not a "free white person." This case, too, was decided in favor of the Armenians, on the basis of racial origins. Ironically, because Armenians were white and Christian, they had been the target of much abuse in the old country; but now this so-called racial status somehow ensured their full legal rights as Americans.

By the end of the era of mass immigration, it was clear that the Armenians had come to stay. They found places for themselves in America and the means to prosper and to build a better life than was possible in the old country. Most of all, the Armenians stayed together, fully intending to continue their life as a people in this place so far away from native lands. The kind of Armenian communities that would grow on American soil would be determined by their conscious efforts to "create the legend" of their lives. ❦

The first generation of immigrants often lived and worked together, softening the pain of being separated from family and country.

FIRST GENERATIONS

The striking upward mobility of the Armenian Americans varied from one place to another. Armenians in the large cities and in California stood a better chance of improving their lot than those who began and remained in the smaller industrial towns. Differences in occupations and in the physical character of these communities dictated different lifestyles. Nevertheless, some common themes bind the experience of the first generations of Armenians in America.

Wanted: Wives and Children

Approximately three-fourths of the Armenian immigrants arriving before World War I were men. Nearly half of these came as bachelors, and the majority of those with spouses left them behind. These estranged husbands often intended to save money and return to Armenia, but as conditions worsened in the homeland, most tried to bring their wives and children over. Legal technicalities made such arrangements difficult until immigration restrictions relaxed after the Young Turk Revolution of 1908. Meanwhile, lonely Armenian men regularly sent money back to the old country, dreaming of the day when their families would be reunited.

Armenians often built their own churches, such as the Holy Trinity Apostolic Church of Fresno, California (pictured here).

The bachelor immigrants faced a greater problem than loneliness: a severe shortage of single Armenian women. If married men had reason to work hard (to earn enough to send for their wives), the young suitors had a similar incentive. The old-country tradition of arranged marriage continued in the new land, and men with good prospects and money in the bank were considered far more appealing as mates. In desperation, some wrote to friends and relations back home, asking that an eligible bride be sent. Such arrangements were not always conducted honestly: Middle-aged men lied about their years and employment, and brides-to-be often proved less skilled or attractive than grooms had been led to believe. Still, to many of the immigrants of the first generations, this scheme was the only choice, for it was unthinkable to join hands with an *odar* (an "outsider," or non-Armenian).

The general absence of families to fill the basic human needs of love and companionship encouraged Armenians to stick together in the New World. In cities and factory towns Armenian men tended to congregate in boardinghouses or to rent rooms from Armenian families. Living near each other, in the same city and neighborhood, even in the same building, fostered the quick growth of a real network of social ties among Armenian Americans.

Comforts Away from Home

Among the first vital institutions established by immigrants were the Armenian coffeehouses. Here Armenian men gathered to relax after long shifts in the factories and fields: to sip Armenian coffee or eat a small meal; play cards or *tavloo* (backgammon); and discuss political and religious issues in their native tongue. Though shunned by Armenian ministers and criticized

Armenian weddings were often long-awaited events. Haiguir Severian married Highganoush Tendekian the very day she arrived in America.

The rituals of the Armenian Apostolic church are rooted in a tradition more than 1,600 years old.

in the press for promoting drinking and gambling, coffeehouses provided companionship for the large number of single men in the Armenian community.

The rapid growth of Armenian-American communities helped stimulate the formation of congregations and church organizations. The first to organize were the Armenian Protestants of Massachusetts, many of whom knew English and had been educated in the American-sponsored missionary schools of Turkey. (After immigration increased dramatically, Armenian Protestants never made up more than one-fifth of the whole Armenian-American population.) Prayer meetings were held on Sundays in American Congregational churches, but because the Protestant community had a small population, the first Armenian-Protestant church building was not completed until 1901. The structure was erected in Worcester with the financial backing of the local missionary society. The first Armenian Protestants of Fresno also received a warm welcome from local Congregationalists —until their minority swelled too close to majority. Then the Armenians were forced to leave the very church they had helped establish in 1883.

Members of the ancient Armenian Apostolic church felt less comfortable worshiping alongside Americans, though some Episcopal churches allowed them to use their chapels for improvised services. Unlike the Protestants, the Apostolics at first had no *vartabeds* (priests) to celebrate the liturgy in classical Armenian. A group of Armenians from Worcester asked the patriarch of Constantinople to send a trained vartabed who could lead them in establishing the first Armenian church in the New World. One arrived in the person of Joseph Sarajian in the summer of 1889, and services were held regularly in rented halls until two years later, when the church of the Worcester parish was constructed and dedicated.

The Soviet Takeover and a Divided Church

The takeover by the Soviet Union in 1921 prompted all Armenians to despair. The dreams of a generation seemed vanquished. Political squabbles revived as the Hunchags and Ramgavars urged acceptance of the Soviet regime and the Dashnags stood their ground on nationalistic principles, accusing Hunchags and Ramgavars of being traitors. Armenian social and charitable events split further along party lines. "Four or five picnics would be carried on simultaneously," wrote Sarkis Atamian, a scholar of the Armenian political parties. As it became all too clear that life in Soviet Armenia would be lived under the dictates of Moscow, the political issue turned into a theological problem as well.

Armenian priests left their homeland to lead congregations in the New World.

The Armenian-American community was shocked by the murder of Archbishop Levon Tourian on December 24, 1933, in the Holy Cross Apostolic Church of New York. This photograph was taken that day.

If the seat of the supreme catholicos remained at Echtmiadzin, in Soviet Armenia, how could the Apostolic church stay clear of the ideological fray and retain its independence?

In 1932 controversy about the display of the flag of independent Armenia at events attended by Apostolic officials provoked several Armenian priests and their constituents to sever ties with Echtmiadzin. The split widened irrevocably on December 24, 1933, when Archbishop Levon Tourian was knifed to death while conducting mass at New York's Holy Cross Church. Several Dashnags were arrested and convicted of the crime, and though the party itself denied any connection to the assassination, Armenian organizations all over America denounced the Armenian Revolutionary Federation (ARF). A faction of pro-Soviet Armenians in Providence retaliated by bombing Dashnag business establishments and murdering several ARF members. Some Armenians have never forgiven the Dashnags for their alleged role in the slaying of Archbishop Tourian, calling them "Armenian Nazis" for their aggressively nationalistic beliefs. Eventually, the anti-Echtmiadzin side formed their own church, the Armenian Prelacy of

America, under the patriarch of Cilicia, who now resides in Antelias, Lebanon.

Armenians today are fortunate that the first generations proved strong enough in number and commitment to survive and even flourish as a divided community. Armenians still shared a common background—and a deep desire to see their heritage passed on to future generations.

Reverend Joseph Sarajian traveled to Armenian communities all over the Northeast urging that local parish councils form and regular services be held. In 1898, the catholicos (supreme head of the Armenian Apostolic church) named Sarajian bishop of the new American diocese, and he continued his pioneering work, setting the stage for the re-creation of the church as the hub of Armenian community life.

Old Questions Arise Again

Churches helped satisfy the Armenian Americans' desire to preserve their native culture. Schools sponsored by the church taught the language and customs of Armenia to the youth born in America. The congregation gathered at weekly services and at holidays such as Christmas (celebrated by Armenians on January 6), Easter, the Feast Days of St. Gregory, and St. Vartan's Day (in memory of Vartan Mamigonian, a warrior who lost his life fighting the Persians for religious freedom in A.D. 451).

The precise structure and function of Old World churches could not be duplicated in the New World, however. Because of a shortage of ordained clergymen, congregations often had to make do with the *kahanas*, or lay clergy, who in the old country received only minimal training to serve as assistants to the ordained priests. When real vartabeds were procured from Armenia, they often found themselves alienated from their parishioners by their ignorance of American ways and insistence on traditional styles of worship. By 1919,

M. Vartan Malcolm, the first historian of the Armenian Americans, mourned falling church attendance and a decided "lack of interest" among the younger members of the community.

Churches also became the battleground for deep-seated conflicts that divided Armenian Americans, who debated the Armenian Question—whether or not Armenians themselves, in the wake of the massacres of the 1890s, should continue revolutionary activities advocated by the political parties. Although much of the Armenian community sympathized strongly with the nationalist cause, the church advocated a more cautious and conservative course. Controversies erupted when priests attempted to discourage party efforts (Bishop Sarajian himself earned widespread unpopularity for censoring a Hunchag newspaper), or allied themselves with a particular faction.

The "rapid turnover" of parish priests described by one historian parallels the pattern of infighting over church matters among New England Puritans of the 17th century. For both groups, a commitment to Christianity as they defined it was central to their long trek to American shores. The bitterness of their internal arguments reveals, more than anything else, just how important religion was to their sense of identity.

The Societies of Compatriots

The networks of friends and families, who often came from the same city or province and then resettled together, formed the vital foundations of Armenian communities in the New World. Many found it exhilarating to meet a childhood pal or former townsman by chance, so many years later and under such different circumstances. The ties of memory helped form these new organizations. Such groups as the Educational Society of Armenian Gregorians of Dodem, founded in Providence, Rhode Island (1891), and the Armenian Educational Society of Pashaghaggee (New York, 1893), sustained a variety of goals, usually including the support of schools and charities in their native villages. Separate literary societies such as the Fresno Armenian Library Union (1890) also sprouted, often with the dual purpose of promoting Armenian culture and helping members to learn English and apply for citizenship.

As word of the massacres reached America, charitable groups quickly organized to aid the orphaned and homeless of Armenia. The Armenian Colonial Association provided essential help to prospective immigrants and earlier arrivals who were down on their luck. Especially effective in overseas aid was the Armenian General Benevolent Union (AGBU), a worldwide organization founded in Egypt in 1908. Transplanted to Boston three years later, AGBU branches quickly took root wherever sufficiently large Armenian communities existed. They collected hundreds of thousands of dollars to assist the needy in their homeland. The Armenian Red Cross, an organization for women founded in 1910, also enlisted a wide membership and made vital contributions to the sufferers.

Keeping an Eye to the East

The desperate needs of the Armenian people in the face of Ottoman persecution, magnified by the personal dilemmas faced by friends and loved ones back home,

Working with the Armenian Red Cross, these women of Worcester contributed to the cause of the Armenian refugees.

riveted the thoughts of the immigrant generation to the Near East and its many problems. Specific crises brought Armenians together in communal enterprises, which surely provided relief from loneliness and homesickness. To understand Armenian-born Americans it is important to realize the nature and strength of their commitment to their homeland. Armenia was the seat of their identity: However grateful the newcomer was for the freedom and economic opportunity of the New World, for those who came before 1920 (while the Armenia of memory still existed) only Armenia could really be home. Thus the ever-volatile po-

Armenians have never relinquished their claim to national sovereignty. Would-be freedom fighter Henry Simonian posed in full garb in 1930.

litical climate in the Ottoman Empire, with its unpredictable effects on the lives of the people of Ararat, was always a matter of great concern. Armenians everywhere sympathized with the yearnings of Turkish Armenians for an equitable system of self-government, if not complete independence.

Moreover, political exiles composed much of the early population of Armenian immigrants. Even a teenager such as John R. Mardick could be incarcerated for such "crimes" against the empire as passing out revolutionary leaflets and running errands for party leaders. Many, young and old, fled Turkey on the verge of arrest for disloyalty. By the 1890s, the two main political groups (the Dashnag and Hunchag parties) had found new footing in the United States.

From the outset, the prime concern of both these parties has been Armenia's political situation. Hunchags began as socialists and supporters of political violence as the best means to achieve Armenian independence. The more moderate Dashnags believed in Armenian nationalism as a unifying force and sought to establish Armenian self-government within the Ottoman Empire. In America, both parties labored to create a free homeland. Toward these ends, the parties sponsored public rallies and Armenian clubs. Like coffeehouses, they catered primarily to men and were scenes of impassioned debate about world politics, Ottoman affairs, and party strategy. These debates grew in magnitude during the years leading up to the Genocide. Basic ideological differences, combined with accusations of blame for the massacres (which on several occasions followed party-sponsored protests), caused the divisions among and within the parties to widen as time passed. The Hunchag party split into "old" and "reformed" factions, while others created the more conservative Ramgavar (Armenian Democratic Liberal) party.

The bitterness of interparty arguments disgusted many. As Robert Mirak has written, the blind zeal of many Old World party leaders, who periodically com-

Armenian-language newspapers kept native culture alive and still provide Armenian Americans with vital links to the past and to each other.

mitted acts of terrorism against other Armenian parties, damaged the reputation of the political activists in America. Yet from the beginning, the political parties played an important role in sustaining a sense of community among Armenian Americans.

The Press: Having Their Say

The patriots of the first generations created and maintained the Armenian press. The first Armenian-language periodical was founded in New Jersey in 1888. Numerous small, independent weeklies and monthlies followed. Few survived without outside financial assistance, and until recent years all the most successful papers have relied on the sponsorship of local or national party organizations. The Boston-area Dashnags created the Hairenik Association, which still publishes *Hairenik* (1899), a daily newspaper, and the Fresno Dashnags founded *Asbarez* (1908), also still in print. These and similar journals passed from hand to hand in clubs and coffeehouses, keeping news-starved Armenians abreast of developments in the the Old World.

Perhaps more importantly, the immigrant press became the bulletin board of community events in America. Their pages featured news about job opportunities, information on immigration, and notices of political and church meetings. A social event that received especially close coverage was Sunday picnics. These picnics combined elements of the ethnic festival with those of the patriotic rally, and they attracted hundreds, sometimes thousands of Armenian Americans, who gathered in a public park for a full day of activities. Like regular political meetings, the picnics were often segregated along party or religious lines. When opponents attempted to make themselves heard, arguments (and sometimes fistfights) resulted. As the years passed, the parties became more likely to sponsor their own social events, their own newspapers, and even their own charities.

Armenian-American picnics served as retreats for families and friends and brought together the larger community.

Despite this absence of unity, Armenian patriots at home and abroad successfully spread word of the Ottoman abuses, awakening many to the immediacy of the Armenian question. In 1917, the Armenian National Union of America sent 1,172 Armenian Americans overseas to help the French army fight the Turks. Members of the Armenia-America Society and the American Committee for Armenian and Syrian Relief (Near East Relief) traveled the length of the country describing the massacres and the plight of the dispossessed Armenians; together they raised more than $30 million. After the Genocide, Vahan Caradashian, a lawyer and prominent Dashnag, organized and ran (from behind the scenes) the American Committee for the Independence of Armenia (ACIA), a lobby boasting the support of such luminaries as Senator Henry Cabot Lodge and Secretary of State William Jennings Bryan. The ACIA pushed intensely but unsuccessfully for direct American aid to Armenia, and later for a U.S. mandate (protectorship under the League of Nations) for the fledgling Republic of Armenia.

Coming in the wake of such unprecedented suffering, independence for Armenia was truly a mixed blessing. Armenians in America celebrated the victories amidst fears that the million refugees within the borders of the tiny republic would soon be overwhelmed by the resurgent Turkish regime of Mustafa Kemal. The Dashnags grew in strength and importance (they were the majority party in the new Armenian government), but the solidarity brought on by the brief Armenian renaissance lasted only as long as independence itself.

Armenian churches remain central to Armenian-American community life. In this photograph women take a break after preparing meals at the Holy Trinity Armenian Church of Boston.

NEXT GENERATIONS

The immigrant generation faced a task even more daunting than the challenge of making a home in a new land: How could the Armenian heritage be passed on to those generations born and raised on the other side of the earth?

Social Roles in and out of the Family

One resource for keeping ancestral links alive was the traditional Armenian emphasis on family life. In the old country, men and women generally considered their lives incomplete if they did not at least marry. Matches were arranged and divorce strongly discouraged. Children completed the proper home life and served as insurance against illness and poverty in old age. Armenians took these attitudes with them to their new homes. Moreover, the witnesses of the Genocide felt it their special duty to ensure the survival of the Armenian people. Immigrant parents dedicated themselves to preserving the values and customs of Armenian life.

Fathers in the New World maintained strong control over the household, earning the respect and loyalty of their families through hard work. Mothers sought to make their dwelling places as Armenian as possible, from the furnishings to the food on the table. Indeed, women played the most important role in transmitting the culture to the next generation, administering the practical affairs of the church, the charities, and the Armenian religious and language schools.

Children, however, had no such clear-cut roles. They were suspended between two worlds: the ways of Armenia, taught by parents at home, and the ways of America, taught in schools and playgrounds from Boston to Los Angeles. The educational system sought to Americanize everyone, and not always in a spirit of kindness and acceptance. William Saroyan, among others, wrote movingly of the prejudice encountered by "foreign" children in the public schools, where insensitive teachers might ridicule everything from immigrant clothing to the contents of an Armenian lunch. The taunting questions of peers told minority children that to be accepted, one had to be as much like other Americans as possible.

In such an atmosphere, conflict between the generations inevitably arose. Children often forgot any Armenian they might have known, parents picked up English slowly, if at all, and a language barrier formed in the household. The ways of the New World, such as unchaperoned dating, mystified the Armenian born. Mothers and fathers reacted quickly and negatively to signs of assimilation, fearing that America, with its open arms, would do precisely what the Turks had failed to accomplish with knives and guns: obliterate the Armenians as a people.

Meanwhile, the second generation searched desperately for ways to both please their parents and build a satisfying life in their own native society. Charles Mahakian, writing 50 years ago, claimed that "the youth . . . attend church not so much for religious reasons as for social reasons." The great question was acculturation (the degree to which one can adapt to a new culture), and there were as many possible answers as there were Armenian Americans. The warnings of the elders and the rebellion of the youth both claim our sympathy. Parents and grandparents lived with a burden of longing, and sometimes an unspoken sense of guilt for having left behind friends, family, and a nation in distress. The problems of the American-born Armenians have roots equally deep. Bred in the years marked by two world wars, in a pervasive atmosphere of patriotic Americanism, they nonetheless have ties to the older generation whose knowledge and experience must always make them "better" Armenians.

There was desire for mutual understanding, but often only time can build a bridge between generations, as David Kherdian has written in a poem entitled "For My Father":

> Our trivial fights over spading
> the vegetable patch, painting the
> garden fence ochre instead of blue,
> and my resistance to Armenian food
> in my preference for everything American
> seemed, in my struggle for identity,
> to be the literal issue.
>
> Why have I waited until your death
> to know the earth you were turning
> was Armenia, the color of your fence
> your homage to Adana, and your other
> complaints over my own complaints
> were addressed to your own homesickness
> brought on by my English.

Daring Young Men: Some Who Made It in the Arts

At times the disturbances and dilemmas faced by members of the second generation have been eased by the grand successes of certain fellow Armenian Americans. The most renowned and inspirational of these is the enchanting and versatile writer William Saroyan (1908–81). Saroyan's fame has been a particular source of pride because his stories and plays present Armenian characters in Armenian and American settings. Born in

William Saroyan was widely acclaimed for his novels, short stories, and plays.

Fresno in 1908, the son of recent immigrants, Saroyan grew up with an intense awareness of the Old World heritage. His first published works appeared in *Hairenik*, the Boston-based paper of the Armenian Revolutionary Foundation, and he continued to write for the Armenian press long after his work became known by a much larger audience.

Saroyan achieved literary fame in 1935 with the publication of a short-story collection entitled *The Daring Young Man on the Flying Trapeze*. The stories in this volume captured the imagination of young and old alike by exploring in a fresh, unpretentious manner many common themes and experiences: growing up "different," the plight of the young artist, and the loss of traditional values in a rapidly changing world. Some of

Saroyan's best autobiographical sketches probe the concept of nationalism, especially Armenian nationalism, in the wake of such shattering events as the Genocide and two horribly destructive world wars. "There is a small area of land in Asia Minor that is called Armenia," he wrote in "The Armenian and the Armenian,"

> but it is not so. It is not Armenia. It is a place. There are plains and mountains and rivers and lakes and cities in this place, and it is all fine, it is all no less fine than all the other places of the world, but it is not Armenia. There are only Armenians, and these inhabit the earth, not Armenia, since there is no Armenia, gentlemen, there is no Armenia and there is no England, and no France, and no Italy, there is only the earth, gentlemen.

With the production in 1939–40 of *The Time of Your Life*, a Pulitzer Prize-winning play, and the publication of *My Name Is Aram*, a group of stories about an Armenian boy growing up in Fresno, Saroyan became a household name and a fixture on the New York–Hollywood social axis. Like many American writers of his time, his work suffered from the harsh spotlight of world fame. While some of his later writings won wide praise (most notably the novel *The Human Comedy*), Saroyan never quite recaptured the grace of his early prose. Nonetheless, William Saroyan's fiction, plays, and memoirs remain a treasure of sensitivity and humor, earning him a place both as a great Armenian and a major American writer. When Saroyan died in 1981, his will stipulated that half his ashes be interred in Soviet Armenia, the other half in his native Fresno.

Armenians take pride in their contributions to the arts in America. One Armenian immigrant who had an incalculable impact on the fine arts in this country is the painter Arshile Gorky (Vosdanig Adoian 1905–48). As a young art student, Gorky saw his entire family perish in the Turkish massacres. He came to America in 1920 and worked at the Hood Rubber Company in Watertown, Massachusetts, until he was fired for painting on the shoe frames. Later, Gorky studied and taught at the Rhode Island School of Design and New York's Grand Central School of Art. His cubist-style drawings and paintings received wide attention when exhibited at the Museum of Modern Art in 1930.

More than younger people could, Gorky felt the pull of the lost homeland. He was particularly proud of the achievement and distinctiveness of Armenian culture, complaining bitterly when strongly expressive details of his paintings, such as his mother's eyes in "The Artist and His Mother" (1926–29), were called Russian or Oriental, when they were in fact Armenian. In the last decade of his lonely, intense life, Gorky pioneered the new style of abstract expressionist painting, in which the canvas is used to express the deepest inner emotions

The sorrows of Arshile Gorky emerge in such paintings as The Artist and His Mother *(1926–29).*

of the artist. Today many of Gorky's works are on permanent display at the finest museums of the world.

Among the young artists taught and befriended by Arshile Gorky was Reuben Nakian (1897–1986), one of the most praised sculptors of our time. During his 70-year career in the arts, Nakian worked in an astounding variety of materials, from plaster to bronze. His efforts were supported by such honors as a Guggenheim Fellowship and a Ford Foundation grant. One of Nakian's best-known sculptures is *Birds in Flight*, an aluminum-on-steel design that adorns the facade of the Loeb Student Center at New York University.

Yousuf Karsh, an Armenian from Canada, is considered to be among the world's finest photographers. Arriving in the port city of Halifax in 1924, at the age

Yousuf Karsh is a world-renowned portrait photographer.

of 16, Karsh worked in his uncle's photography studio and showed such talent that he was sent to study with John Garo, an accomplished Armenian-American portrait photographer. After setting out on his own, Karsh won quick acclaim. His celebrated photo of Winston Churchill, printed on the cover of *Life* magazine in 1940, established Karsh as the Mathew Brady (the renowned Civil War photographer) of this century. Since that time, Karsh has been in constant demand to photograph popes, premiers, presidents, and prizewinners, always seeking "to stir the emotions of the viewer and lay bare the soul of the subject."

Rouben Mamoulian, another immigrant who made a lasting contribution to the visual arts, won praise as a stage and screen director. Born in Soviet Armenia at the turn of the century, Mamoulian got his big break in 1927, when he directed the first Broadway production of the play *Porgy*. He later oversaw the production of the operatic *Porgy and Bess*, which featured a score by George Gershwin. Mamoulian's other stage works include first runs of the musicals *Oklahoma* (1943) and *Carousel* (1945). Yet Mamoulian's greatest impact has been in the field of cinema. He was the first director to mount the motion picture camera on wheels and the first to use more than one microphone, innovations that revolutionized the possibilities of perspective in film. Classic films directed by Mamoulian include *Dr. Jekyll and Mr. Hyde* (1932), *Queen Christina* (1933), and *The Mark of Zorro* (1940).

For more than a millennium, music has held a special place in Armenian culture. Armenian chant, or church music, developed independently of Byzantine and Western forms and still plays a prominent part in the Armenian rites. Armenians especially appreciate the works of Alan Hovhannes (born in 1911), a widely recognized Armenian-American composer who has often been inspired by traditional Armenian melodies and themes. Born in Somerville, Massachusetts, Hovhannes achieved substantial success in the 1930s writing in the vein of his conservatory teachers, then decided to start all over again, burning all his previous scores. He worked for seven years as an organist at the St. James Armenian Church in Watertown, Massachusetts, and studied eastern music and philosophy. Since that time, Hovhannes has been invited all over the world to conduct his colorful, expressive pieces. These include more than 60 symphonies (mostly for small orchestras), such as *The Mystery Mountain*, named for Mt. Ararat, and the *St. Vartan Symphony*. Like Nakian and Karsh, he has remained artistically active well into his senior years.

Leading the Community

Armenian Americans are fond of noting how often their Old World specialties have led to success in the New World. The Armenian passion for education is today best personified by Vartan Gregorian. Born in Iran in 1935, Gregorian studied at an Armenian college in Beirut, Lebanon, and received a scholarship to Stanford University in 1955. Nine years later, with a doctorate in history, Gregorian embarked upon a career as a teacher, scholar, and administrator. Appointed professor of history at the University of Pennsylvania in 1972, he served as dean of the faculty, and provost, leaving in 1981 to become president and chief executive officer of the New York Public Library, the second-largest free library in the nation. Gregorian has succeeded in raising funds for much-needed repairs and renovations at the Research Library, which receives more than 1.5 million visitors each year. He has also overseen the implementation of a computer search system that will eventually catalogue all the library's holdings, so that library patrons may more easily, in his words, "transform information into knowledge."

Like many other ethnic groups on the American scene, Armenians have also prospered by introducing their foods to American palates. Armenians were the

Vartan Gregorian, an Armenian from Iran, serves as president of the New York Public Library.

The philanthropy of Alex Manoogian (wearing hat), founder of the Masco Corporation and president of the Armenian General Benevolent Union, has been an inspiring example to the Armenian-American community.

first to market yogurt (*matzoon*) in this country. Peter Halajian and several friends parlayed an Armenian candy-peddling venture into the Peter Paul Candy Company, makers of the York peppermint patty and the Mounds and Almond Joy candy bars. George Mardikian (1902–85) founded the renowned Omar Khayyám's Restaurant in San Francisco, specializing in traditional Armenian dishes such as shish kebab, pilaf, dolma, kuftehs, and paklava.

After World War II, Mardikian advised the U.S. Armed Forces on improving soldiers's rations. Overseas he encountered thousands of dispossessed Armenians who, because of their political affiliations, feared to return to Soviet Armenia. As related in his touching memoir *Song of America* (1956), Mardikian founded the Armenian National Committee to Aid Homeless Armenians (ANCHA), to help sustain and eventually resettle the new Armenian refugees. ANCHA is still operating and has played an important role in the relocation of thousands of Armenians from the strife-torn Middle East. George Mardikian received the Medal of

Freedom from President Eisenhower for his patriotic and humanitarian efforts.

Another young man who fled the massacres and became a leader in the Armenian-American community is Alex Manoogian, founder of the Masco Corporation. Manoogian, who arrived here in 1920, became a multimillionaire after inventing the Delta single-handled faucet. Known for his exceptional generosity, Manoogian has donated millions of dollars for the establishment and support of Armenian schools and cultural foundations in the United States and Canada. Since 1953 he has served as the international president of the Armenian General Benevolent Union.

The Armenian Americans have produced a number of prominent entrepreneurs, but none has amassed power and fortune as shrewdly as Kirk Kerkorian, chairman and controlling stockholder of MGM, Inc. Born in Fresno in 1917, Kerkorian developed a passion for planes, serving in Britain's Royal Air Force during World War II. Within a few years after opening his own flight school, he bought and restored several planes and transformed his small enterprise into Trans International Airlines. Eventually he sold Trans International, acquired Western Airlines, and made incredible sums of money speculating in the booming real estate market of Las Vegas. In 1974 Kerkorian took over Metro-Goldwyn-Mayer, where he oversees enterprises as diverse as film production and the construction of luxury hotels such as the Las Vegas MGM Grand.

Public service has attracted a number of Armenian Americans, particularly in the state of California. Charles (Chip) Pashayan, a Republican now serving a fifth consecutive term, represents the Fresno district in the House of Representatives. The most visible Armenian American on the national scene today is George Deukmejian, governor of California. Deukmejian was born in Menands, New York, in 1928, and grew up in an Armenian family he described as marked by "closeness and discipline." After studying sociology and law at Siena College and St. John's University, and spending three years as a lawyer in the U.S. Army, Deukmejian moved to Long Beach. He won a race for the California State Assembly at the age of 34 and has not been out of office since. He was elected state senator in 1966, attorney general in 1978, and governor in 1982. Four years later he scored a second consecutive victory over Tom Bradley, the popular mayor of Los Angeles. Considered a conservative Republican, Deukmejian is best known for his strong anticrime stance and his aggressive budget-slashing measures. He has been mentioned in political circles as a potential future presidential candidate.

The capstone of a career in public service: George Deukmejian after his inauguration as governor of California in 1983.

In America politics often resembles athletic competition, another area in which Armenian Americans have performed well. Ara Parseghian coached college football at Miami University of Ohio and at Northwestern before the "era of Ara," his 11 consecutive top-10 seasons at Notre Dame (1964–74). Parseghian now provides commentary for network sports telecasts. Garo Yepremian, an Armenian from Cyprus, was one of the first soccer-style placekickers in the National Football League; his bald pate and uniform number became a familiar sight during the Miami Dolphins' championship years in the 1970s. Currently, relief pitcher Steve Bedrosian of the Philadelphia Phillies overpowers National League batters with a fearsome fastball. He made the All-Star team in 1986 and 1987, and in 1987 earned the Cy Young Award as the best pitcher in the league.

A Worldwide Community Tries to Relocate

The achievements of this group of first- and second-generation Armenian Americans characterizes the experience of the entire community. Armenians in America have earned success in fields as diverse as the fine arts, big business, education, sports, and politics; yet their commitment to self-advancement, some argue, has worked against the Armenian community. Like most Americans, Armenians' individual efforts to serve their ethnic community usually take a backseat to personal goals. Still, few members of the group have ignored the pressing needs of less fortunate Armenians struggling in other parts of the world. The renewal of immigration since World War II has provided transfusions of new blood into communities, reminding many Armenians that collective needs must be addressed if they are to survive as a people.

The rigidity of American immigration laws in the mid-20th century helped shape a distinct Armenian community in Canada. The original Armenian pioneers

In 1987 Steve Bedrosian garnered the National League Cy Young and Fireman of the Year (awarded for best relief pitcher) awards.

of the northern lands were the Dukhobors—Russian Armenians who arrived around the turn of the century, some of whom later moved to California. Other groups, including many orphans, came after the Genocide. The Canadian-Armenian community numbered only a few thousand until the 1940s and 1950s, when many fled the Middle East and the political upheavals of Eastern Europe. Aided by the Canadian Armenian Congress, thousands settled in or near Montreal and Toronto. The total number of Armenians currently living in Canada probably exceeds 50,000.

In the ensuing years, immigration to America also rose in response to international crises. Civil war in Lebanon during the late 1970s prompted thousands of Armenians there to move west. An even more perilous situation forced Iranian Armenians to flee their native country after the Ayatollah Khomeini's radical Islamic regime seized power. In 1981 alone, 2,500 came to America. Finally, a relaxation in immigration policies has permitted many Soviet Armenians to come to North America. Although only a handful had previously been allowed to emigrate each year, a total of 311 Soviet Armenians were permitted to leave in the single month of June 1987.

Differences between the new immigrants and the second- and third-generation Armenian Americans have led many to declare the new arrivals "a different group altogether." Nearly all the new immigrants speak Armenian, and most confess to puzzlement about what they perceive as the indifference of Armenian Americans to the mother tongue and the mother church. Often the newcomers dismiss the majority of Armenian Americans as assimilated, "shish kebab" Armenians.

A majority of the new Armenians have settled in California, especially in Los Angeles County, which now claims the largest proportion of Armenian Americans in the nation. The Soviet Armenians in Hollywood, for example, have developed into an entirely separate community 35,000 strong, with schools, churches, and social centers distinct from those of other Armenians. The newcomers even speak a dialect, peculiar to Eastern Armenia, that varies considerably from Western, or Turkish, Armenian. "They come from a different system," explained a reporter from the New York Armenian press who interviewed area residents. Their common experience in a society quite different from America makes it natural for them to cling together, as did the Turkish-Armenian immigrants of a century ago.

Assimilation, as always, presents a most complicated issue to Armenian Americans. The old solidarity within their community has been shaken somewhat by growing diversity. New immigrants strengthen the church, the schools, and the life of the language, yet simultaneously serve to divide the community by locale, origin, and experience. Community leaders are hopeful that both groups will eventually conclude that what joins the new and old Armenian Americans is greater than what pushes them apart. ∾

ARMENIAN AND AMERICAN

Despite problems rooted in generational, geographical, and ideological differences, the Armenian-American community survives as a tremendous resource, especially for those members who live in or near Los Angeles, New York, Boston, Fresno, Montreal, or other areas with relatively large concentrations of Armenians. A total of about two-thirds of a million Armenians live in North America, and though this number is impressive, it constitutes only a fraction of one percent of the continent's total population. How does the relatively small size of the community affect Armenian Americans?

Fighting the Stereotypes

Ignorance on the part of others is the first obstacle to a comfortable existence as an Armenian American. "It is no easy thing to go through life," writer and educator Marjorie Housepian once commented, "having to explain, at every turn, just what an Armenian is." With ignorance comes insensitivity. Many Americans recognize Bastille Day (which commemorates the 1789 French Revolution), the Chinese New Year, St. Patrick's Day (the annual tribute to Ireland's patron saint), and know something about the foods and dress of many nations, but precious few are familiar with the Armenian Apostolic church.

Even the Genocide remains a shadowy event in the minds of most Americans. Some older citizens recall the phrase "the starving Armenians" used in the relief fund drives of the 1920s; some wonder if any Armenians survive. For the past 70 years, Armenians everywhere have had to cope with a prevailing stereotype of Armenians as "Turk-haters." Worse, few people understand the cause and character of the Genocide. The Turkish government maintains that the "alleged" bloodshed never happened, that the Genocide actually consisted of a series of minor insurrections and a mutually agreed upon resettlement program. Armenians are torn between a commitment to spreading the truth about the 1.5 million martyrs and a desire to avoid losing the present in anguish over the past.

Another form of prejudice faced by Armenian Americans today is the "rug merchant" stereotype based on the domination of the Oriental carpet industry by Armenian Americans. Their subsequent success in other business enterprises contributed to an unflattering stereotype of Armenians as wily, aggressive, greedy salesmen. A recent incident provides a good example of such bigotry in action. In 1984, Jerry Tarkanian, head basketball coach of the University of Nevada at

Armenian refugees lined up to thank Americans for their support of Near East Relief during the massacre years.

Armenian Americans annually gather to protest the Turkish government's denial of the Genocide. This Armenian Martyr's Day march took place in New York City in 1975.

Las Vegas, was suspended by the National Collegiate Athletic Association for multiple rules violations. Afterward he sued for libel. During the trial, one of the defendants (an investigator for the National Collegiate Athletic Assocation) repeatedly referred to Tarkanian as a "rug merchant," until he was reprimanded by Judge Paul Goodman: "Mr. Tarkanian is the plaintiff, Neil Manouikian is the chief justice of the Nevada Supreme Court, and the governor of California is George Deukmejian. And there is not a rug merchant in the lot." Armenians, like members of other ethnic groups, often enter society with one strike against them and must strive to overcome crude misconceptions.

The Fight to Retain an Identity

Prejudice has led many American immigrants to shorten or change their names: Karnig Elvasian became Carl Sivas; George Elmasian became George Mason; Mardiros Fereshtian became Mark Fresh. Sometimes a new name implies a denial of one's original identity. Consider the case of Michael Arlen (1895–1956), a best-selling novelist in the 1920s and 30s. Born Dikran Kouyoumjian in Bulgaria, he moved to London at the age of 18. The young Kouyoumjian, as his biographer Harry Keyishian has written, felt much despair at the status of his exiled people, who possessed a heritage without the support of a land, a center. Arlen wrote in his first book, *The London Venture*: "An Armenian, who

Soviet-Armenian wrestlers perform a traditional dance before competition.

soon realizes his nationality is something of a faux pas. . . . is entirely lost in the wilderness, for their is no solid background to his existence in another's country." He later chose to ignore Armenian themes altogether and soon earned an international reputation for *The Green Hat* and other novels that satirized London high society. One popular story has it that Arlen was asked by an inquisitive lady: "Are you really an Armenian?" Arlen supposedly replied: "Madame, would anyone choose to be Armenian?" Arlen, who thought it hopeless to retain his ethnic heritage, repeatedly warned his son of the danger of getting "too close" to fellow exiles.

Arlen came to maturity as a man and a writer in an era of strident, exclusive nationalism. Today we live in a different world, one in which ethnic differences are more likely to be accepted, if not always appreciated. A genuine revolution in social values occurred in America after the 1960s: Gradually, ethnicity became a cherished source of pride. This change in attitudes stemmed partly from the civil rights movement, which highlighted the isolation faced by minorities in this country, especially blacks. For groups who came to this continent by choice, the ethnic revival included a reaction against earlier trends toward assimilation. The new generation, and often the second generation as they reached the middle years, began to believe that by cutting themselves off from their ancestral links they deprived themselves of something worthwhile. They began to think that ethnic heritage was perhaps something to be celebrated rather than overcome.

John Hagopian remembered feeling hampered by the old-fashioned ways of his immigrant parents. But despite marrying a non-Armenian, he wrote: "The older I became, the more Armenian I became. . . . I guess I read a lot of Saroyan." Leo Hamalian, a writer and professor at the City College of New York, also experienced a revolution in outlook regarding the meaning and value of his Armenian-American identity:

> I myself once felt the weight of what I interpreted as opposing obligations, the Armenian and the American. But now I believe that my ethnic background has broadened and deepened my perspectives on almost everything that touches me.

In the 1970s, many Americans embarked on a mission of rediscovery, looking inward and to the past in the hope of gaining a sense of their own roots. Michael J. Arlen, son of the novelist and himself a writer, published a narrative of his encounter with his Armenian heritage entitled *Passage to Ararat* (1975), that became a best-seller and won the prestigious National Book Award. In his book, Arlen outlines his difficult relationship with his Armenian heritage and also with his father, describing how he gradually began to accept both. On one occasion, he was asked to speak at New York's St. Vartan Armenian Cathedral, a place he had never before visited:

> Such small beginnings. That evening, for the first time, I met Armenians on my own. Armenian women who laughed and asked too many questions. Thick-chested men who seemed always to have their arms around each other. Too many cups of coffee and small, sweet cakes. I was *there*—wherever *there* was. It was an uncertain beachhead, for I kept fighting off the desire to bolt. Never let them get too close! But I also knew that a corner of some missing piece had briefly become visible.

"People aren't afraid to be foreign anymore," a member of an Armenian dance group told a reporter from the *Wall Street Journal.* In other words, one could be an Armenian without lessening one's identity as an American.

The Triumph of Ethnicity

Once ethnicity had become accepted as a positive force, Armenians undertook a large-scale cultural revival. Old organizations gained strength, and new institutions took root as never before. Even the call for language study, unheeded for so long, found supporters. Churches offered programs in Armenian language, culture, and history. Full-time, accredited day schools, some taking students through high school, came into existence, founded and supported by individual donations. In 1987 more than 20 such institutions flourished. Although only a small percentage of Armenian-American children attend these schools, the number has steadily risen in recent years.

In the past two decades Armenian culture has won recognition from American institutions of higher learning. The National Association of Armenian Studies and Research helped start college courses in Armenian, and graduate programs in Armenian studies are now offered at such prestigious schools as Columbia, Harvard, and the University of California at Los Angeles (UCLA). California's American Armenian International College, associated with the University of La Verne and now in its 11th year, has become a center for studies in Armenian culture.

Particularly encouraging to those concerned about the next generation is the level of involvement by the young. The Federation of Armenian Student Clubs of America has chapters at 60 colleges. Political and benevolent unions are active, but the most popular program in recent years has been the annual Armenian Olympics, with competitors from all over the United

States and Canada gathering in California for track and field, basketball, and volleyball tournaments.

Further evidence of the community's vitality is the *Armenian-American Almanac* (1985), the first of its kind, which lists charitable and social organizations, schools, publications, and so forth. There remain a number of active compatriotic societies and numerous clubs devoted to Armenian art, dance, literature, even coins. In California and New York, there are Armenian Citizens' Leagues and an Armenian Network that regularly bring together Armenian professionals and business people. Seven homes for retired persons serve hundreds of elderly Armenians.

The largest Armenian organizations serve mainly charitable purposes. The Armenian Students Association, founded in 1910, consists largely of groups of alumni who raise funds for scholarships. The AGBU sponsors concerts, lectures, publications, and educational projects, as does the Knights of Vartan, a nationwide fraternal society. Armenian secular groups thrive in the new atmosphere of ethnic revival.

An increasing number of applicants have been allowed to leave Soviet Armenia for the United States. In October 1987 this group lined up at the U.S. embassy in Moscow to apply for exit visas.

George Mardikian welcomed these homeless Armenians to the United States in 1961. The Committee to Aid Homeless Armenians still assists many victims of the Armenian diaspora.

The Armenian church, however, has not experienced such unqualified success. Attendance continues to drop; leaders worry even more about the split in the Apostolic church. Today North America has 117 Armenian churches: 5 Armenian Catholic, 24 Evangelical (or Protestant), 30 belonging to the Armenian Apostolic Church of America (or the Prelacy), and 58 pledged to the Armenian Church of North America (or the Diocese). Though relations have improved between Armenian Protestants and Apostolics, years of negotiations between the two opposing Apostolic groups broke down in 1986. A group called the Coalition for Church Unity has pressed for an end to the disunity, which has wrought severe damage, especially in New York, where the eastern headquarters of both the Diocese and the Prelacy function within half a mile of each other.

Armenians still regard the church as essential to their heritage. This does much to explain the strenuous conflicts of the past and present: Those involved have always cared enough to argue vehemently for their vision of the role of Armenian religion. Individual churches act as a unifying force, bringing whole communities together on holidays. Church buildings double as community centers, constant reminders of the roots of Armenian culture and the path of Armenian history. Sometimes they even serve the larger community, as in the case of the St. Vartan Armenian Cathedral and Cultural Center in New York. Each year the church and the city cosponsor the One World Festival, a celebration of crafts, music, and foods from all nations.

The state of the Armenian press is another fair gauge of community activity. In 1987 there were 15 Armenian-American newspapers, 5 of which printed solely in English, and 9 journals and magazines, (of which 3 ran all their articles in English). Some of these publications serve as organs of the political parties: the ARF's *Asbarez* (Fresno), *Hairenik* (Boston), and *Armenian Review*; the ADL's *Armenian Mirror-Spectator* and *Baikar*. The AGBU publishes *Ararat*, a literary quarterly, and *Hoosharar*, a monthly bulletin. The emergence of several independent weeklies, most notably New York City's *Armenian Reporter*, has heartened many Armenians who believe that progress toward unity must come from new sources. Though naturally biased in favor of unity and against the party interests, the *Reporter* does serve as an open forum, reporting "all the news about Armenians," printing letters, historical articles, and book reviews, and providing a calendar of events in the Northeast.

Armenia: Hostilities at Home and Abroad

The Armenian press remains the battleground for a host of unresolved controversies. More and more Armenian Americans have come to accept the Armenian Soviet Socialist Republic as the true Armenia, taking vacations there and working for cultural exchange. Meanwhile, the international Armenian Revolutionary Foundation continues to demand an independent Armenia within the old boundaries. The "tricolor question" resurfaces constantly. Followers of the Echtmiadzin patriarch view the flying of the flag of free Armenia as a deliberate insult, and the vehemently anticommunist Dashnags object to the hammer-and-sickle symbol on the Soviet-Armenian banner.

The community has cohered around the issue of Turkey, which refuses to admit the truth of the massacres. On two occasions, Turkish representatives to the United Nations vigorously objected to the inclusion of the Armenian tragedy in reports issued by the Sub-Committee on Genocide of the United Nations Commission on Human Rights. A large proportion of articles in the Armenian press are devoted to the status of the Genocide in the mind of the world: Ignorance must be fought if a recurrence of the mass murder is to be prevented. The prospects for a coming to terms between Armenians and Turks, however, have been dimmed by violence on the part of frustrated Armenian nationalists. In 1973, Kikran Yanakian, an 80-year-old Armenian man, shot two Turkish diplomats in Los Angeles. Since that time, periodic incidents have forced Armenians in the United States and Canada to question the nature of revenge and the nature of justice.

In 1975, in Lebanon, an international terrorist organization called the Armenian Secret Army for the Liberation of Armenia (ASALA) dedicated itself to world recognition of the Genocide and the liberation of Turkish Armenia. Over the past 12 years, the ASALA (which is supported by the Palestinian Liberation Organization) has taken credit for attacks on scores of Turkish officials, including the bombings of embassies and consulates in Los Angeles, Toronto, and Ottawa. The problem of Armenian terrorism came even closer to home in 1982 when a similar group called the Armenian Revolutionary Army, which includes at least several American members, murdered the Turkish consul general in Los Angeles. Though such attacks on innocent individuals were condemned by community leaders, donations by Armenians provided bail for the suspects in the bombing case. No Armenian organization has endorsed terrorism, and all worry that the media coverage generated by these attacks may injure the public image of Armenians in America and Canada.

Despite these incidents, most Armenian Americans have concentrated their efforts on peaceful protest. The Armenian Assembly, founded in 1972, lobbies in Washington, D.C. In recent years, Armenians have sought congressional recognition of Armenian Martyrs' Day (April 24) as a "National Day of Remembrance of Man's Inhumanity to Man," condemning genocide and all acts of bigotry. The cause has not won universal support in the federal government, however. The Turkish government has repeatedly threatened to sever ties with the United States and perhaps jeopardize American missile placements in Turkey if the measure is passed. Though the resolution has twice achieved a ma-

jority in the House of Representatives, the Reagan administration has worked hard against its passage, contending that such recognition would "legitimize terrorism" and "harm relations with an important ally."

For the fourth consecutive year, in 1987 the Martyrs' Day resolution failed to pass, but this did not prevent many states from issuing proclamations. On April 21, 1985 (the 70th anniversary of the execution of Armenian leaders in Constantinople, marking the onset of the Genocide), Armenians gathered by the thousands at Times Square in New York City and at Arlington National Cemetery for commemorative ceremonies. The event has been repeated in New York and in other cities during the past two years. For Armenian Americans, the Genocide adds up to more than a historical tragedy; it remains the shaping event of their lives, and the reason they came to fashion a new life on a new continent. To ask that they forget is to ask them to forget who they are.

The flame at the Monument to Victims of the Genocide in Yerevan, Soviet Armenia, burns eternally to commemorate Armenian martyrs.

One Community Among Many

The Armenian-American community continues to redefine itself. Renewed immigration should ward off further loss of traditional ways, and the tendency of the new immigrants to live together ensures that some ethnic communities will grow for years to come. The decline of nativism makes it easier for ethnic Americans to practice openly the ways of their forefathers. At the same time, though, American society encourages intermingling and assimilation. Some leaders estimate that more than half of young Armenian men and women are marrying non-Armenians, making transmittal of the heritage an urgent problem.

To some Armenian Americans, the real difficulties stem from problems within their own population. Jack Antreassian, a writer and editor, protests that "our organizations and institutions . . . magically drawn over themselves the mantle of Armenianism, rendering any criticism of them tantamount to treason against the ancient heritage of our entire nation." Pride and sensitivity discourage prospective members of the community organizations; for Antreassian the "Ten Commandments of the Armenian Community" seem to include "Thou Shalt Not Criticize," "Thou Shalt Keep Thy House Divided," and "Thou Shalt Not Bow Down to Any but the AGBU." Some wonder if the tremendous waste of resources exemplified by the competing churches and parties will not slowly drain the strength of existing bonds. Yet the heated nature of the arguments surely reveals how heartfelt is the commitment to the survival of the Armenian people.

Members of ethnic groups may be joined by a variety of geographical, cultural, racial, historical, and religious ties. Armenians are often bound by all of these. The separate nature of Armenian churches—Catholic, Protestant, and Apostolic— reinforces a strong sense of ethnic identity: a past, a language, an ancient homeland. Through centuries of dispersal, the Armenians have retained these common bonds; through generations in America they have kept and nurtured a dual identity. They remain Armenian and American. ❧

FURTHER READING

Antreassian, Jack. *Ararat: A Decade of Armenian American Writing.* New York: Armenian General Benevolent Union, 1969.

————. *Definitions and Deflations.* New York: Ashod Press, 1984.

Arlen, Michael J. *Passage to Ararat.* New York: Farrar, Straus & Giroux, 1975.

Baliozian, Ara. *The Armenians: Their History and Culture.* New York: Ararat Press, 1980.

Hamalian, Leo. *Burn After Reading.* New York: Ararat Press, 1978.

Kherdian, David. *The Road from Home: The Story of an Armenian Girl.* New York: Morrow, 1979.

————. *Finding Home.* New York: Greenwillow, 1981.

Lang, David Marshall. *The Armenians: A People in Exile.* London: George Allen & Unwin, 1981.

Malcolm, M. Vartan. *The Armenians in America.* Boston: Pilgrim Press, 1919.

Mardikian, George. *Song of America.* New York: McGraw Hill, 1956.

Mirak, Robert. *Torn Between Two Lands: Armenians in America 1890 to World War I.* Cambridge, MA: Harvard University Press, 1983.

Saroyan, William. *The Saroyan Special.* Plainview, NY: Books for Libraries Press, 1970.

INDEX

Picture Credits

We would like to thank the following sources for providing photographs: AP/ Wide World Photos: pp. 70, 88, 92; Courtesy Armenian Library and Museum: pp. 15, 31; The Bettmann Archive: pp. 23, 82; Stephen Ferry/St. Vartan Armenian Cathedral and Cultural Center: p. 94; Kirkorian Family Collection, Balch Institute for Ethnic Studies: p. 96; Library of Congress: pp. 27, 28, 42, 44, 46; Kenneth Martin: pp. 54, 55, 56; MAS: p. 17; Matenadaran Manuscript, 1569: p. 16; New York Public Library Picture Collection: pp. 24, 87; New York Times Pictures: p. 101; Project Save: pp. 26, 69; Project Save/Courtesy of Armenian Revolutionary Federation: pp. 19, 57; Project Save/Courtesy of Ara Avakian: p. 66; Project Save/Courtesy of Vincent Beck and Mrs. Leon Podg: cover; Project Save/Courtesy of Maria Bashian Bedikian: p. 32; Project Save/Courtesy of Betty and Charlotte Calfaian: p. 73; Project Save/Courtesy of Dr. H. M. Deranian: p. 58; Project Save/Courtesy of Reuben Gregorian: p. 20; Project Save/Courtesy of Ardashess Hampar: p. 18; Project Save/Courtesy of Rose Dermenjian Haroutanian: p. 78; Project Save/Courtesy of Jack Kachadoorian: p. 77; Project Save/ Courtesy of Suney Kachadoorian: p. 47; Project Save/Courtesy of Mary Avadanian Kachichian: p. 60; Project Save/Courtesy of Shinork Kilarjian: p. 33; Project Save/ Courtesy of Margaret Kedonian Melickian: p. 36; Project Save/Courtesy of Mary Melilian: pp. 64, 74, 75; Project Save/Courtesy of Alice Gulanian Papazian: p. 63; Project Save/Courtesy of Highanoush Fendekian Serverian: p. 67; Project Save/Courtesy of Satenig Tashjian Simsarian: p. 39; Project Save/Courtesy of Suren Stevens: p. 40; Project Save/Courtesy of James Tashjian: p. 97; Project Save/Courtesy of Marie Iskian Tevonian: p. 34; Herb Snitzer Photography: p. 53; Sovfoto: p. 13; Mark Stein Studios: p. 14; Tass from Sovfoto: pp. 98, 105; Katrina Thomas: pp. 49, 50, 51, 52, 68; UPI/Bettmann Newsphotos: pp. 85, 90, 102; Whitney Museum of American Art: p. 84

DAVID WALDSTREICHER is a 1987 graduate of the University of Virginia, where he studied history and English literature. A winner of the Mellon Fellowship in the Humanities, he is currently enrolled in the doctoral program of American Studies at Yale University. This is his first book.

DANIEL PATRICK MOYNIHAN is the senior United States senator from New York. He is also the only person in American history to serve in the cabinets or subcabinets of four successive presidents—Kennedy, Johnson, Nixon, and Ford. Formerly a professor of government at Harvard University, he has written and edited many books, including *Beyond the Melting Pot, Ethnicity: Theory and Experience* (both with Nathan Glazer), *Loyalties,* and *Family and Nation.*